Contents

ARTISTS

THOMAS SAYERS ELLIS

Windows, Open Homes, A Sense of Community

For the most part things happen when they are supposed to, when a combination of characters and conditions make it possible. I didn't discover *Agni* until issue #29/30. I knew of its existence, but do not recall seeing it until then. The first thing I did was glance down the table of contents looking for familiar names. I found two among many. Uneasy at first, I remember that there were names I had never heard pronounced, whose pronunciation I couldn't be sure of: Akhmatova, Rymurak, Scialabba. I also remember thinking it contained a lot of writing. Not too much, just a lot. Dilemma: should I sit a long time with it, or have many sits? Its size alone challenged me. A relationship had begun.

Issue #33 was the first time my work appeared in *Agni*, but by then I'd become an outside family member, a half-brother who on holiday visits listened and watched very closely from other rooms. The publication was and still is very dear to me because I remember feeling like I was becoming a part of a dialogue very local and at the same time very global: Chomsky, Moldaw, Salamun. Back issues, like photo albums, gave me a sense of *Agni*'s breadth and history, its community.

There's no doubt about whether or not I have since come to view the journal as a home—a great many writers do, some I have met, some I will never meet. *Agni* is the kind of home whose rooms I am comfortable in. I am comfortable that if I feel a chair or painting is in the wrong place it can be changed. I am comfortable with being close enough to be both recognized and heard. At the same time, I am comfortable with the reality that the rooms exist to comfort more people than myself, democratic by design, open.

I don't remember who it was that described to me the poem as being a home and stanzas as being rooms. What I do recall is that the analogy changed the way I saw into writing, my own as well as others. Once that door was opened for me, I was able to enter and find the windows. I was able to look out, turn, look in. This is where, surrounded by family members, I got the confidence to accept such an endeavor as editing a supplement of young poets.

Why us? I think we were picked because we were, and to some extent still are, the type of individuals who as kids always brought friends and stray animals home. "Mom, can this person stay over?" and "Dad, I found a kitten. Can I keep it?" We share the same common desire to include and discover as many voices as possible. The same is true of Askold Melnyczuk who chose us. And like those kids, who ultimately discovered the family couldn't take in or feed every friend, we were forced to exclude. "Standing on the Verge" turned out far more competitive than either of us imagined. A great many good poets were rejected and friends turned back. We chose work that surprised us, work filled with windows and bridges, the kinds of strays and friends we'd still bring home today. We argued, disagreed, discovered things about ourselves only time will heal, read, re-read, listened as the submissions shaped the supplement, as our creative processes intervened in selecting poems and their order. Joseph rode the bus to Boston. I rode the bus to Providence. Our apartments became jungles of large red rubber bands, jiffy bags and *Agni* stationery. Poems hung from our refrigerators, "Must remember to show Lease these." We read a lot, piles and piles for months. "I'm still excavating it all."

February, 1993
Cambridge, Massachusetts

JOSEPH LEASE

Start From Where You Are

For every comparison, there is an axis of difference and an axis of similarity: every generation differs from its predecessors in some ways (as it reinvents them), and resembles them in other ways (as it reinvents them). If, as Yeats said, out of our arguments with ourselves we make poetry, the young poets in "Standing on the Verge" can start that argument from pretty much anywhere, can frame that argument in such diverse ways as to be almost unprecedented in their inclusiveness.

Starting from anywhere. Certainly this group of poems feels like it has the power to start from anywhere: any subject can start the poem; any speech act or kind of figurative language can start the poem. There is greater diversity—of experience, of voice, of aesthetics—here than in most anthologies; perhaps this is due to the character of the generation represented here, as well as to the society they inherit and contest.

Perhaps, if these poems are young, it is in that they search out extremes, of voice, of experience—as poetic events, their needs are palpable. Sometimes the voices in these poems embody the fundamental questioning of life and of identity which has so often made youth into a storm in our culture. Many of these poems tend towards outrage, many others of them toward investigation; often, these poems appear not to be surprised by anything, but that mask soon slips, as well it should. Whatever else these poems are, they are surprising, demanding, generous and searching. Their real and imagined struggles are complex and fertile. Often they end by demanding a further investigation—yet another reimagining of their subjects— by the reader. Combining image and voice, exploring lyric structure and personal and social conflict, they give the first experience of a world that is still ahead of most poetry being written today.

My deep gratitude to Askold Melnyczuk and D. M. de La Perrière.

February, 1993
Providence, Rhode Island

Silver Queen

The stuffed hedgehog whose snout melted
on the radiator wore the same overalls checked shirt
had the same bristly hair as Mr. Beavenhauer
who grew vegetables behind the stores that sprang up
long after he established his rhubarb and asparagus
with a dollar each we hunted him down among
his potatoes dusty brown shoes heels flattened no laces
once we saw him in a suit he had a gold watch
but maybe that was a dream because that old car
he idled by our kitchen Margie I've got fresh beans
and my mother wiping her hands huddling with him
over heaped boxes but maybe he *was* rich because
when we found him dwarfed by corn stalks he felt
for full ears stripped back husks to let us look
white pearls gold silk he piled my arms high
always more than we asked for he took our dollars
and gave my sister change always more
my mother said than enough.

Indian Paint

It was a heart attack that knocked Bill Yeagley flat of course
he smoked but still I thought arthritis because I'd overheard
how it stiffened him so he'd start down the steps and then
be seized and turned like something blowing amazed
to arrive at the bottom on his feet after that
I watched for him I spent a lot of time on the
curb peeling bark from his sycamore hunting
soft stones at its base you could make bright
powder by scraping them on cement he called it
Indian paint he had a copper ball to plug in
and put his hands on when they hurt so he got
thinner and thinner I looked up from my stones
he took a few steps and then ascended like a
leaf I looked back my dust scattered orange
and red the trees the whole neighborhood
transformed.

Uncle

You're not afraid are you
big girl like you I was watching
their horse mouth hay he and my father stall
in the shadows I wasn't listening except to
the horse's jaw except when he said
that because earlier the way
he reached for me yes
I was afraid.

Blue Willow

A pond will deepen toward the center like a plate
we traced its shallow rim my mother steering
my inner tube past the rushes where I looked
for Moses we said it was a trip around the world
in China we wove through curtains of willow
that tickled our necks let's do that again
and we'd double back idle there lifting
our heads to the green rain
swallows met over us later I dreamed
of flying with them we had all the time
in the world we had the world
how could those trees be weeping?

KEVIN YOUNG

Clyde Peeling's Reptiland in Allenwood, Pennsylvania

You must admit it's natural
that while waiting for the three o'clock
informational reptile handling & petting

show, we all imagined a few choice tragedies,
maybe a snake devouring one of the six
identical blond children in the front row,

or the anaconda choking on all five
badly braided girls. I confess openly
we discussed ways in which the obnoxious

crying child in the third row actually wriggled
free of daddy's constricting arms, his head opened
against the ground like a melon & a ripe one

at that. See, in the end the tragedy is all
in the telling, not at the moment when the gator
slips out of Ched Peeling's trusty, thoroughbred

hands & gobbles down a few select
youngsters—preferably the really loud or
beautiful ones—but later, after the ambulances

have sped away & no one breathes
a word. Even when everything is said
& done, I don't know whether only the loud

& really beautiful things get remembered
or most things just grow loud & beautiful
when gone. I can only tell you

that later I thought for hours about Irvy
the Alligator's smooth underbelly & the way
it drove him nearly extinct, how folks once

looked at him & called him desire, a handbag
in waiting. How you won't drive past any Negrolands
on your way through Pennsylvania, or anywhere

else in this union. How while learning about lizards
that grow their tails back, bloodless, I kept
thinking The Colored Zoo may be exactly what

we need, a pleasant place to find out how They eat
watermelon & mate regularly, a cool comfortable
room where everyone can sit around

& ask *How do I recognize*
one or protect myself? or *Their hair,*
how do They get it to clench up

like that? A guide dressed in unthreatening
greens or a color we don't have to call
brown could reply *Good question,*

then hold one up & demonstrate, show
all the key markings. But you must
believe me when I say there is not really

such a place, when I tell you that I held
my breath with the rest at Reptiland, listening
to Ched recite his snakebite story for the four-

hundredth time, waving around his middle finger
where the rattler sunk fangs. You must forgive
how we leaned closer as he described venom

eating green & cold through his veins, pictured
perfectly its slow nauseous seep, like watching
the eleven o'clock footage of someone beaten

blue by the cops, over & over, knowing you could
do nothing about this, only watch, knowing
it already has all happened without you

& probably will keep on happening, steady
as snake poison traveling toward the heart,
the way these things go on by, slowly,

an ancient turtle we pay
to pet as it walks past,
souvenir, survivor.

Everywhere Is Out of Town

for Maceo Parker & the JB Horns

Beanville. Tea
party. Five black cats
& a white boy. Chitlin
circuit. Gravy-colored suits,
preacher stripes. Didn't
know you could buy
muttonchops these days.
Afros. Horns slung
round necks like giant
ladles. Dressing. Uptempo
blessing: *Good God*

everywhere! We bow our
heads before the band
lets loose. Drummer unknown
as a hymn's third verse.
Older woman pushes toward
the front, catching the spirit
like the crazy lady at church
six scotches later. Communion

breath. Hands waving. Sweaty
face rags, post-sermon
mop, suicidal white girls crying
like the newly baptized. All that
water. Play it. Swing
it. *Be suggestive.* Request
"Chicken" & "Pass the Peas"
like we used to say. Have mercy!
Thanksgiving's back in town

& we're all crammed in the club white
as the walls of a church basement. Feet
impatient as forks. Only ten bucks
a plate for this leftover band. Thigh,
drumsticks, neck. Dark meat.

GABRIELLE GLANCY

In Visible Light

1. IMPASSE

Even though I was there I could go no further

The imagination is dark—
                    —and predatory

and like a constellation
has its own

logic

I see
There is no link
between

what I was and what I saw

2. TURNING AWAY

If we look ahead
we see

we will have to look back

Ask yourself: what frightens you?

Even at the expense
of

identity may not find itself
through relationship

3. CONFLUENCE

If this refusal of the world
If this turning inward and away
      from conversation

If this looking-at and gathering-in

Then I am the migratory
      birds

I am
sky, I am
the Mississippi river
girl's lifted hands
birds, sky, migrating, refusals
I am outside
and inside, you
world—as—it—is

EDWIN FRANK

Portrait

That coolness—

A myth—of nymphs
Sprawling at the hidden
Sources, their limbs
Coiled or outstretched, clear beneath the still
Dark water—

Of a god, newborn—

Though I was a weak
Dull boy, my dry
Papery skin a phosphorescent white.
I didn't know the word for anything.
I didn't have a gift for anything.
I rode my bike,
Twisting and struggling, up and down the block.
The training wheels squeaked—

Sleep-sundered, motherless:

Here are the red mud
Houses I built
Along the river, the bitter
Mineral smell, the sweet
Sudor of growth, mild decay,

Snapped roots sticky with dirt, clogged
Superflux of
Wormlife brooding,

Behind each door;

And here are the small
Exquisitely crafted
Gold-leaf panels
I have suspended
From two ropes running
From the floor to ceiling—

Old things out of—

For the fire without witness—

I was king of that ditch.

LAURA MULLEN

The Castle

I refused to believe I was
Pregnant.

Pregnant or just before a storm,

Purely local.

And the limp bodies of the young women
Are wheeled out, drooping, and lifted
Up by the men to be dropped on the beds
Where they lie for a while, inert
And faintly crying. As in a science-
Fiction film.

I just felt sick all the time.

◆

It's the body you can't get to,
Even though it is yours.
Nominally yours.
For a little while.

◆

The nurse saying *Hush, hush.*

◆

Eyes shut, lying flat
As though sleeping, a woman
Traces with the tips of her fingers the shape

Of her bare breast.

There was a room that opened up
Into another room.

She shuts her eyes tighter.

A room that opened up into another room
Opening up to a big
Picture window.

Lines
In the skin around her eyes from the force
Of her closing them, *tick, tick.*

The rooms empty, the picture window blank.

◆

And wasn't it beautifully furnished?
Magnificently:
There was nothing you could touch.

House

Where the winds cross
Where the currents meet
                    (This voice came to me)

House of wind or water
Shifting

Sliding in and out of

Shape. "I . . ."—
Where for an instant. . . .

Where perhaps for an instant. . . .

◆   ◆   ◆

And then I thought the warmth I felt, in the dark, clear, deep, bitterly
salty and cold water—it went all the way down, this sudden warmth—
was something dangerous: another body, resting on the bottom (waiting),
or, because I knew by then the canal was polluted, some kind of toxic
waste; I went that far, in my fear, yes; the edges of it (that heat) were so
distinct. And knowing the fear was crazy, but not being able to shake it
off—"probably crazy"—wanting out, and not even being sure the
sensation was real (intense sensation that could have been pleasure, if I
could have . . .): not being sure I wasn't making it up.

◆   ◆   ◆

Voice which came out of the silence.

                                        A "silence"

Held in place:
The sense of there being no place for anything other

Than the dutiful return
To the picturesque.

♦ ♦ ♦

The mountains on the other side,
Clear-cut.
Patches of thin green, new growth, and the three
New dark red gashes,
"We can't do anything about,"
A wave of the hand towards the view from the table,
"It's in another county."

Carried easily over the water all day the dense sound
Of gears changing to take the steep grade,
The trucks heavy.

♦ ♦ ♦

Intermittently,
Afloat,
Leaves, twigs, grasses,
The cobweb-fine meshes
Of bright green moss.

Near the shore
The white splotches of empty
Oyster shells gleaming up
From the bottom.

Four seals in the distance I was also
Frightened of.

(Changed, in my dream,
To four sharks—
Which *waited:*
Had *intention*, lurked. . . .)

But the scar across my ribs,
In the mirror, later, where I was

Peeling away the wet black suit,
Was a strip of seaweed, merely—
A fake wound—
Which also came off.

◆　◆　◆

House taking shape and collapsing.
"Not trustworthy."

> (That last the most constant
> Voice or the voice
> Most constantly trusted.)

◆　◆　◆

Not looking at the actual
Mountains (which had been
Spoiled) but at their
Reflections in the water,
Or learning to see them
As, at dusk,
Lovely shapes: violet–
Blue between the gold sunset
And the silver water.

Sheer mass we watched—our faces
Close to the glass to shadow
The mirroring window—a private
Display of fireworks
Burst out, show up, against.
In silence.
On that side it was night already.
But we had to look carefully, to keep
Our glances lowered: the last
Light above the jagged peaks
Still blinding.

◆　◆　◆

I wanted to stay,

Was trying to stay

(Up in the slight warmth of sunlight, merely: you could see, still, the whole
White length of arm and leg)

On or at least near
The surface:

Careful. Good. Safe.

The attention to beauty, to detail. Something
(Large) rotting away or wrong (waiting)
Underneath.

◆ ◆ ◆

Silence.
Or the voice that said Why live.

And the words drained of meaning,
Specifically "love."

◆ ◆ ◆

"Not trustworthy."

◆ ◆ ◆

Blues, greens, golds, and the light off the water
Imitating water
Across the red brick of the fireplace, the bare wooden walls:
A golden net, swaying, which dissolved
And lifted clear again, shifting, from moment to moment,
Never still. . . .

Which faded away as the sun went down.
Which faded away slowly as the sun went down.
Which faded away,
Went out,
As night set in.

The rhythms—
Found out in the effort
To fix it—so seductive: the illusion
Of something being prolonged or held back.

As if you could put it on "pause" forever,
Flickering slightly, but staying:

As if you could open up the instant before
And live there,

In the inevitably belated
"As if it hadn't yet. . . ."

As, for instance, with the accident. . . .

(But you pointed out how, in trying to locate it, whatever "'before'" was
((that fault)), the place where it could have been halted or made to
happen differently, kept getting further and further away, kept going
back, out of reach, like the roots of the horsetails, which had "taken over":
everything too entangled—a network—and going down too deep.)

As, for instance. . . .

◆ ◆ ◆

In the clear cut beside the road where the skid marks. . . , the shatterproof
Glass lay like blue ice, in summer, across the jagged top
Of a redwood stump, and glittered among the dead
Branches and small broken trees which had been
Not worth it,
Evidently.

Darkness also
Slowly closing over that.

◆ ◆ ◆

But not a surface,
Unbroken;
Not a skin,
Closed off.

◆ ◆ ◆

I had a sense of things as fragile,
Myself as well,
Threatened, but also
Part of the threat.

A sense of things as held in place
With some effort: an agreement,

And an urgency to the pretence
Of there being nothing urgent.

◆ ◆ ◆

Up in the sunlight layer, buoyant, staying as close to the surface as I could
get, I was still a moving break in the tension, I could tell, a hole (in that
mirror), a gap, a betrayal, a dark place. Wondering what whatever it was
that was at the bottom was reading me as. A shape. "Afraid."

◆ ◆ ◆

I got up and went for a walk
Along the narrow strip of beach the tide
Had given back. The rocky beach,
Littered with oysters and empty
Shells, a flowing line of green leaves
And broken twigs, moss and grasses,
Running the length of it, high up
On the steep bank. It was still
Very early; the light silvery, pale;
No one else up. I went out on the dock
And sat on the sprung diving board,
Looking out.

I was trying, this time, to get past
"Guilt," which wasn't enough, anymore,
Which was a way, I thought, of keeping
Something always between the actual
Event, and the image—
I was holding onto, of myself—

It shattered.

Oh, not exactly "perfect."
A laugh. The small waves, made up
Of wind and current, slapping lightly
At the dock, the reflections
Shifting, I'm not talking about that.

But I could see how I had managed,
By being "guilty," by my expressions
Of grief and shock and self-disgust,
To keep (the outlines
Rippled but inviolate) a sense of someone
"Good enough," or rather, "almost
Good enough"
To go on living.

(Someplace *distant.*)

But I could no longer afford
The cost of the two
Establishments. . . .

The picture
I had had to break
Myself
To keep intact.

◆　◆　◆

Maybe the dark
Green on the sides of the silvery
Waves was a chance to look in,
For once: the actual color:
The lid of a box, opening up
And shutting. . . .
A glimpse,
Borne towards me and swept past,
Of a possible house.

(Long grasses swayed there gently,
Together and apart, the vacant
Shells glimmered up, bone white, and three
Crabs clung to a ragged shred of fish—
Each one frantic to both eat and keep
The thing—so that it fairly waltzed
Across the sand, the unwilling feast:
A jerky, halting dance, the gestures
Broken down into abrupt
Fragments. . . .)

CARL PHILLIPS

A Mathematics of Breathing

I.

Think of any of several arched
colonnades to a cathedral,

how the arches
like fountains, say,

or certain limits in calculus,
when put to the graph-paper's cross-trees,

never quite meet any promised heaven,
instead at their vaulted heights

falling down to the abruptly ending
base of the next column,

smaller, the one smaller
past that, at last

dying, what is
called perspective.

This is the way buildings do it.

II.

You have seen them, surely, busy paring
the world down to what it is mostly,

proverb: so many birds in a bush.
Suddenly they take off, and at first

it seems your particular hedge itself
has sighed deeply,

that the birds are what come,
though of course it is just the birds

leaving one space for others.
After they've gone, put your ear to the bush,

listen. There are three sides: the leaves'
releasing of something, your ear where it

finds it, and the air in between, to say
equals. There is maybe a fourth side,

not breathing.

III.

In my version of *One Thousand and One Nights,*
there are only a thousand,

Scheherazade herself is the last one,
for the moment held back,

for a moment all the odds hang even.
The stories she tells she tells mostly

to win another night of watching the prince
drift into a deep sleeping beside her,

the chance to touch one more time
his limbs, going,

gone soft already with dreaming.
When she tells her own story,

Breathe in,
breathe out

is how it starts.

Becoming Miss Holiday

If you can't be free, be a mystery.
  —Rita Dove

You're no mystery, really.

Mornings of no particular sky, and
alone, so that it seems all the
same whether I remove my clothes
or merely let it be understood,

by baring the sunlessly pale
shoulder, by leaving the neck
open to whatever nails the rain
may let drop in its passing,

that I'm prepared to do so, I
step with your pulled–to–crack
notes from room to hourless
room, free the windows,

test the air's give. I
clutch the radio's staticky
blooms to my chest,
I say here's

how the gardenia surrenders.

SUSAN HALLAWELL

Eighth Grade Acrostic

Candi leaned so far into the porcelain hole
Her knee touched the drain. Passing
Lip gloss and blush as if it were wine
And wafers, she could reach the only
Mirror by bracing herself on urinals,
Yellowed and cracked since the old seminary
Degenerated into our middle school.
I read aloud vocabulary from health posters
As Candi drew her lips. *Chlamydia, menses.*

In one pamphlet, the vaguely romantic: *fellatio.*
Sins, even our worst, were elevated by Latin.

Not that I could always trace the derivation.
Orgasm was an enigma. Candi claimed
That, like *sodomy*, it was Greek. And not a sin.

A *seminary*, I knew, was a nursery. A garden.

Five minutes each morning, in the break between
Language Class and Homeroom, we bowed
Over urinals to fix our hair and faces.
We studied more than semantics, we were
Engaged in ritual. The lavatory was history,
Religion. The words became our own.

Testimony of the Female Serial Killer

He ground a row of white–green worms
under his heels,
lit a match and burned
one live. It made me almost feel

like crying. Men can be cruel
but they're too small to ever take
it back, even the one who
said he loved me, that snake

broke my windows with his fist
wrapped in a towel,
then claimed he'd slash his wrists
if I left. How

could I let him live?
To be honest, this last guy,
I didn't really give
a shit about those worms. Why

I did it was he made my skin
crawl—his fingernails and hair,
even his come smelled clean.
Deep down inside they're

the same, I know—all
sour with blood;
smeared on the motel walls,
it's just handful after handful of mud.

PETER MARCUS

The Insomniac's Pet Shop

I have no use for cages.
They can copulate wherever
they want. By moonlight, I clean
the dead canary of the birdseed
it is lying in. Pluck the pretty
feathers—the azures and the yellow—
greens. I keep one sign facing
inward: Thank you. . . Come Again. . .

The SPECIAL OF THE MONTH
is rat and roach
for lovers of the scuttle
and the heavy gait. With Chopin
on the antique phonograph
I savor the skips and scratches;
waltz with the white toy poodle
who sleeps in the wire cell by the window.

In my pet-shop, the fish tank
is covered with a hairy-green
algae no one can see though.
To buy a goldfish from me
is an act of faith. And maybe,
like your own prayer for rest,
you'll hear the tiny diver
calling you from the bottom.

To Hear the Chorus Sing

A man alone in the middle of his bed.
His penis rising because it loves
to rise, regardless of what the man does
or does not love. Shifting like a compass
arrow that points to the forest
he never tires of discovering. Pointing
upwards to remind him to love
the rest of his body:
his small unnourishing nipples,
the Apple in his throat that stops
his song like a stone. As he touches
himself he defies himself; remembers
the luminous mallard clamping the duck
with his bill and the dragonfly—
long turquoise needle of light
crazed and sizzling pushing her
in delirious circles around the sky,
coyotes crying from hill to hill,
a barn owl carrying in its voice
the first memory of water.
He senses what moves
from the stomach, what dips
into the testes, what sings upwards
is not the blood, but light,
reaching for the farthest walls
of space and never reaching them.
And when desire quiets
he settles back into himself
like the sleek crescent moon
into daylight. Knowing this form
was chosen for him,
he curls into himself,
holding his animal body like a mother.

PAJA FAUDREE

Awake

Sheets
twist and heat
    the damp boy. The window swims blue,
    angry, wild eye: *Sleep. You*
        must sleep. In boxes baby cows,

deep
in fat, sleep
    When the boy dreams, it is of eggs
    breaking, shell by shell. Legs
        of cockroaches scratch bare floor. Light

slips
in cracks, drips
    like a leaky faucet, around
    the door, wave on wave, pounds
        the boy. Today he heard cows' sighs

lift
like scabs, sift
    sand across the delicate skin
    of his ears, cries as thin
        as dying, flaming leaves. Windowed

tree
spears cleanly
    the voiceless moon. It helps to think
    of throwing eggs, that blink
        like eyes, against the wall, one by

one.
The yolks run,
      melted fat. Not much help. Shadows
      scrape the walls. The hollows
            of his bones vibrate with the baby

cries
of cows, wise
      with pain. His plastering clothes trap
      him awake. Ruthless map
            of light finds him. Baby cows, he

thinks and cannot sleep.

Lefty

Friend, you want to make lace
and your only tool is an ice pick.
Know, then, that your palms will open,
the weave may never close,
the result may be pegboard
or chicken wire or Swiss cheese.
Know that no one believes
in lace anymore,
that the few who do
can sew better than you.
Know this: another yard of lace
won't change anything,
but oh, how vibrant
and well-built the light
that enters
through the clumsiest holes.

PAUL BEATTY

That's Not in My Job Description

despite that i overslept
and set a guinness book world record for coming in late
its still time for me to take my 15-minute break

pull off my sweater vest
talking shit

cross my sneakers on the desk
threaten to call my union rep
if these fools

                dont stop lookin at me crazy
                whisperin lazy
                under their breath

but on my siesta
i eavesdrop on societys best

                    imagine im a distinguished ethnographer

on the black pbs
talkin with a british lisp
in front of a bookshelf

welcome to alistair cooke's *In Search of*
today we pursue The Elusive True Nature of Whitey

                        notice as
                        our cameras
                        zoom in on

a pinstriped pack of business school well groomed brooks brother
    smoothies
encamped around a water cooler   jostling for room in their natural
    habitat
wiping dunkin donut crumbs off their jackets and engaged in debates
on hot topics
such as:

        nuclear waste   the china syndrome
        alternative methods of heating their homes

                                        and right before

                    the herd starts to roam

        the menfolk take part in the ritual
        shooting of the stryofoam cups into the trash basket

and if they make it
they dance around like
they just saved the world

headin my way
lookin for some dap
so i try to look busy
which im good at

start rustlin charts
construct some new paper clip art
chew on a pen cap   as if   im seriously studying my messenger map

hmmmm did you know that main street runs perpendicular to beech
            and parallel with elm for exactly I and seven/eighteenths of
            a mile before it intersects with west crest
            well blow me down

i aint got time to mope
worryin aloud about
how imma cope wid radioactive isotopes and mushroom clouds

when its me myself
                              thats about to explode

an overloaded low level gung-ho ah–so nigro rickshaw coolie
the company dr. doolittles thought they knew me
i talk the animals   como se llama   push–me–pull–me

bowin n kowtowin
eatin crow
holdin my tongue
hands clung so tightly to the bottom rung
cant even reach for the glass ceiling

                              my feet planted in corporate dung

        growing roots
                    in the ground zero
                                    terra firma
                        of affirmative
            daily inaction

                    copy xerox mop   remember the blues ones go on top
                    shred fedex the checks   press the red button next
                    fax wax collapse   the green mail sacks go to jack

right after i put my year-end evaluation
in the management trainee mailbox

one of them fresh out of college cookie cutter fuckers
invites me to meet the buddies for drinks at mcgillicuddy's

i only wanted a nine to five
that classified didnt say nothin bout havin to socialize

now this wage slave
is t-minus nine heinekens from critical mass

        me and a few hoogie white democrats
        drinking after work rolling rock
        smoking marlboros out the box

all you can do is wait for the chain reaction show of ass

when one of em
looks me in the eye
                and decides
                        to say something to the colored guy
its
all systems go
the white folks start actin like they know

                hey bro er uh bro—ham
                i happen to be a big rap fan
                went to see ice cube and michel'le
                at the hollywood palladium
                and i was the only white person in the place
                aint i soul brother

there must have been another workshop on how to handle your
        support staff
which in this craft is a euphemism for niggers n spics

itsa trip
watching a one-sided will to unite

if i could get in a word edgewise   i wouldnt
                                         since im with my boss
                                         and dont want to get fired
                all i can do is sigh
                                         too chicken to pay the price

as they get excited
giddy from overexercising their rights

my dad owns a liquor store in the inner city   so i know how you feel

ive read toni morrisons beloved twice
and eventhough i still didnt get it the second time   shes just so real

i believe that spike is truly five for five
no no you dont understand   i really want to be like mike

or maybe a harlem globetrotter
its my dream to send my daughter to spelman
where can she get a check up for sickle cell
whats the name of your hair gel/pomade
do you use a depilatory when you shave
how can i join the crips
just *what is hip*
i know its after the fact but i dont think king should called for calm
i wanna be a minister in the nation of islam
isnt so and so such an uncle tom

when theyre through
they pat themselves on the back
and quote jesse jackson

*we have to start on the front end of head start and day care
not on the back end of prison and welfare*

keepin hope alive
i buy the next round

wonderin how it would sound if i changed my name to skip
placed a mike tyson kingsized if i ruled the world chip on my shoulder
went to a joint full of the rednecks
put my elbows on the bar cleared my throat and said

becks
then id go into my show

did you know i was elected to the senate inna landslide
and i was the only colored man there without rag in my hand for
polishin brass or shining shoes

or

at last weeks tractor pull i was the only spear chukker
drivin monster pick-ups over a bunch of crushed oldsmobiles

or

i sailed in the americas cup

or

i went to the university of vermont   and rowed crew

or

i grew up in a two room shack in the appalachian mountains picked
myself up by the shitkickers went door to door selling berlitz and
scripture moved to utah sang soprano in the mormon tabernacle choir
married into the osmonds and now i spend my weekends smokin pot
with donnie and marie reading back issues of teen beat magazine

or

im included in the canon
im a cardinal in the vatican
im the highest paid player on the boston red sox
i own IBM stock
i play nazi punk rock
i drink coors extra gold by the case
i can say puke with a straight face
i have a seat on wall street
im an LL bean catalogue model
my art is in the metropolitan
i had a major part in a woody allen movie
and i do the broadway casting for tommy tune

but i wouldnt give a shit about nuna dis
if i could just say   im a nigger who has enough room

Your Mouth Near My House

Come alone, past the sacred argument
Of winter. Do not rely on the broken
Glass of stars. It was an elaborate

Mistake the night you happened to look up.
Now you cannot stop approaching; it holds
Like the last edge of sunset, all that fire

Emptying itself against the coming dark.
In the rough silence my fingers
Devise a pearl, a bald jewel, the color
Of hope. I watch for your mouth, the door

Opening to my ruthless house
A man and woman forgot they had built.
It should have been a cave, carefully marked
By those who had been, and you still to come.

Among the Divided Lilies

(ICU Waiting Room, New York 1984)

I.

Too late, I saw the body,
I compared. Either unlucky
Or clumsy with desire it lies
Wheeled against the wall, ready
To be sent for. An arrow
Elaborates the way out. The angel
Stayed only as long as the life
Was solvable. Not so much
Waiting as listening, not so much
Witness as spy, I sit on blue
Upholstery and read the pamphlet
Again. Key points have been marked with
Stars: honesty, night sweats, patches that look
Like bruises. Such is the new precision.

II.

One by one the houses
Closed their doors: too risky.
I hold nothing against this holiness
But the snake of an old wound.
Whatever sickness exists
Is now in the hands of others
Confirmed and public. There is the noise
Of people who hear nothing
But the latest results as they walk
Back into their life. And what is
Leftover survives the long reproach
Of new blood laddering through veins—
It becomes a wise wound, a chalk circle,
Bullseye. Oasis, a place where gathering begins.

III.

How simply the cathedral turns
Inside out: here's the steeple
But no door through which
The body comfortably fits.
Those left behind are busy
Guarding immunity
In a locked chest. They believe this
As their lifework. Be careful what you do
Unto others, gloves and masks upon
Entering. Cover the head, kneel
In the aisle, never with a short skirt
Or shoulders bared. Remove jewelry
And watch for blood, any sign of blood.
It is a river that refuses to be easy.

IV.

The face of the doctor
Learns to turn into a field
Of gray rock. It has seen too much:
No more shame in hesitating
Against what disappears. Yet his hands
Of repair continue their science
And he will send the white
Messenger with a tricky blur
Of either paradise or grief
To the bone. Stiff plastic curtains
Groan back into place and weary
Promises drip toward random dread. Do not
Move fast. Do not let yourself grow angry.
If you stay still long enough someone will find you.

V.

A day will happen
When I can no longer visit;
From nowhere I will wake up
Finished with vigilance
And go through each room
To make sure each face
Does not look like mine.
Against these blank walls,
Among the divided lilies,
Beside the high fidelity
Television, I will stop asking
The question and head down
The illuminated stairs, making a way back
To Arrivals and the suddenness of traffic.

Like Sabines

She woke on the forest floor
wondering about the trees,
about their growing being more

of a digging in and pushing
up from the roots, up from what she was
taught was the forgiven earth.

Where was the water now?
Where were the scars? Perhaps too far down.
Down between her legs she remembered

feeling something wet, remembered
being thirsty, being forced down
where she could really see the trees,

where she believed heaven begins,
where the uppermost leaves finally gave up,
where the little bits of blue show through.

Perhaps he was up there now she thought,
and his penis—some thing like the trees,
some thing that she never saw growing

but was suddenly there, big and hard
before her—perhaps it was in hell,
perhaps the judging, transporting angels

decided to consider them as two
different animals. He wasn't all bad,
wasn't really bright, yet seemed so different.

Though he was the same age as the others
he seemed so much younger. She didn't know
that he wanted what all the other boys wanted

when he asked her to walk with him,
because the others didn't really like
to have him hanging around.

She noticed that he laid her down,
almost gently, his body was beautiful,
and his pants were below his knees.

His breath in her face kept her still.
It smelled like a drug store or a what not shop,
more of chocolates and mint Lifesavers,

nylon stockings, hard rubber combs, lint
brushes, and toothbrushes than drugs, more
of witch hazel and wrinkle cream.

Aisle one is for deodorants.
Aisle ten is for toilet tissue and laundry
detergent she thought as she tried to freeze,

act uninterested, not go into shock
as he did it to her. There you could buy
perfume, and lip gloss, plastic beach balls,

cheap toys that may entertain a child
for an hour before being thrown away
with broken springs. He had a penis,

and a knife, and his kisses seemed like questions.
She wondered if she could say something
and change his mind, send him away shriveled.

She thought she could move her bowels
or simply say Bobby I know your father,
but even then he could keep pulling up

at her dress. So she lay there with the rocks
at her back and his hands on her breasts

and from the wooded ground she thought
that this was at least better than death.

SUZANNE KEEN

FROM "A Psalter"

ps. 4

Friend, marauder, neighbor,
        fellow–dweller,
eavesdropper,
        reader, cellar-lurker,
jimmier of locks:
        will you help me
keep still in my chamber?

For a brief time,
        she carried a twist
of flesh, flesh
        of his flesh,
blastula turning in
        on itself, signature
of a compact from which
        I was excluded.

Poor little flicker
        of a thing,
I imagined you
        in the form of a chicken
embryo, all albumen
        and burgeoning yolk,
nicked countenance,
        and pulse.

Friend, marauder, neighbor,
        fellow–dweller,
eavesdropper,
        feeder, cellar-lurker,
jimmier of locks:
        will you tell me

to be still in my chamber?

He said your mother
          looked at the screen
involuntarily,
          that she was sorry.
You did not meet
          your evil godmother
or receive your
          silver-plated gifts.

I imagined you licking
          the window and
looking at me
          through the tongue mark,
while your mother
          was digging
with an ivory hook
          to retrieve a dropped stitch.

Friend, marauder, neighbor,
          fellow—dweller,
eavesdropper,
          reader of no meters,
jimmier of locks:
          will you let me
stay still in my chamber?

          In my chamber
I wished you were still.

Boat, he reads,
        bead, bed.
He levels
        a sheet
precisely,
        under
each of the
        quelled words.

Together,
        we read
a story,
        "They save
money at
        the store."
Buy in bulk.
        House brand.

François writes
        to me.
I read what
        he prints,
answering
        how he
saves money
        on food.

Dear Suzanne,
        I drink
the water.
        I don't
buy the juice.
        He signs
in cursive,
        François.

Abundance
            devours
from within.
            The tongue
roars, caught in
            its pit,
sounding out,
            and stuck.

He labels
            pictures
until *goat*
            is left,
and the blank
            under
the plate, knife,
            fork, spoon.

Which one is
            the meal,
I ask him.
            He says,
I tell you,
            if I'm
hungry, I
            would eat
him.

ps. 8

What game did the baby-sitter teach us?
                It was Witch in the well.
It went this way: you be the witch. Get in
                the fireplace, where the gas
burner was. You be the mother. Someone
                has to be the girl.
The mother tells the daughter, "Go get water
                from the well." The daughter
goes to the well. There's a witch in the well.
                The mother gets angry.
"Just get me water out of the well!"

                There's a witch in the well.
The mother must stay just around the corner.
                She must raise her hand to strike.
"If you don't get me water from the well!"
                The third time is the last.
The witch comes out of the well for the girl.
                Then fly around the house.
The witch goes after the girl. The mother
                goes after the witch.
This game is played without water. Someone
                has to be the girl.

What was the game that I was teaching him?
                I was sucking his tongue.
I wasn't pretending anything then.
                I was latched onto it.
Where did the nipple come from, the steep slope
                of breast, a canopy
curving heavily away from the pole?
                Surely not from thin air.
Heavens, moons, stars, and he disappeared,
                covered, become breast.
Which one was drawing water from the well?

This game was played within water. Someone
                had to be the girl.

The Alzheimer's Monkeys

for J.B.

My friend who knows says they exist,
rare prizes in the research labs
where I imagine them slumped in cages,
dumbfounded by the slightest banana
and drooling on their immigrant nurses
who lead them in the sensible shoes
of science to a cold table with straps.

My friend says the problem is time:
slow changes over fifty years see
the scientists grow feeble and thin
until they're too confused to open
the cages. My friend, who never wonders
what he is doing, says his own lab
backed away, preferring instead
the smart monkeys who know they are dying.

On Hearing About the Disappearance of Frogs

How shall I make them up?
Or tell my daughter (now herself
a frog) that by streams in the summer
I was less alone?

I'll say steps used to echo in water,
algae used to have eyes, that one is born
into missing families who teach us
to hold our breath in the womb.

I've heard it all before, she'll say,
and keep walking, moisture beading
her forehead, mud webbing her toes,
legs alert to a shadow.

Her eyes go back to water.
Her sleep rises up from the mud.
And the Buddha with his frog-grin
is the prince she cannot kiss into air.

HARRYETTE MULLEN

FROM "Muse & Drudge"

Fatten your animal for sacrifice, poet,
but keep your muse slender.
　　　—Callimachus

1.

sapphire's lyre styles
plucked eyebrows
bow lips and legs
whose lives are lonely too

my last nerve's lucid music
sure chewed up the juicy fruit
you must don't like my peaches
there's some left on the tree

you've had my thrills
a reefer a tub of gin
don't mess with me I'm evil
I'm in your sin

clipped bird eclipsed moon
soon no memory of you
no drive or desire survives
you flutter invisible still

2.

another funky Sunday
stone-souled picnic
your heart beats me
as I lie naked on the grass

a name determined by other names
prescribed mediation
unblushingly on display
to one man or all

travelling Jane
no time to settle down
bee in her bonnet
her ants underpants

bittersweet and inescapable
hip signals like later
some handsome man kind on the eyes
a kind man looks good to me

3.

I dream a world
and then what
my soul is resting
but my feet are tired

half the night gone
I'm holding my own
some half forgotten tune
casual funk from a darker back room

handful of gimme
myself when I am real
how would you know
if you've never tasted

a ramble in brambles
the blacker more sweeter juicier
pores sweat into blackberry tangles
going back native natural country wild briers

4.

country clothes hung on her all and sundry
bolt of blue have mercy ink perfume
that snapping turtle pussy
won't let go until thunder comes

call me pessimistic
but I fall for sour pickles
sweets for the sweet
awrr reet peteet patootie

shadows crossed her face
distanced by the medium
riffing through it
too poor to pay attention

sepia bronze mahogany
say froggy jump salty
jelly in a vise
buttered up broke ice

5.

battered like her face
embrazened with ravage
the oxidizing of these
agonizingly worked surfaces

that other scene offstage
where by and for her he descends
a path through tangled sounds
he wants to make a song

blue gum pine barrens
loose booty muddy bosom
my all day contemplation
my midnight dream

something must need fixing
raise your window high
the carpenter's here
with hammer and nail

6.

sun goes on shining
while the debbil beats his wife
blues played lefthanded
topsy—turvy inside out

under the weather
down by the sea
a broke johnny walker
mister meaner

bigger than a big man
cirrus as a heart tack
more powerful than a loco motive
think your shit don't stink

edge against a wall
wearing your colors
soulfully worn out
stylishly distressed

Naola Beauty Academy, New Orleans, Louisiana 1943

Made hair? The girls here
put a press on your head
last two weeks. No naps.

They learning. See the basins?
This where we wash. Yeah,
it's hot. July jam.

Stove always on. Keep the combs
hot. Lee and Ida bumping hair
right now. Best two.

Ida got a natural touch.
Don't burn nobody.
Her own's a righteous mass.

Lee, now she used to sew.
Her fingers steady
from them tiny needles.

She can fix some bad hair.
Look how she lay them waves.
Light, slight and polite.

Not a one out of place.

Drapery Factory, Gulfport, Mississippi 1956

She made the trip daily, though
later she would not remember
how far to tell the grandchildren—
Better that way.
She could keep those miles
a secret, and her black face
and black hands, and the pink bottoms
of her black feet
a minor inconvenience.

She does remember the men
she worked for, and that often
she sat side–by–side
with white women, all of them
bent over, pushing into the hum
of the machines, their right calves
tensed against the pedals.

Her lips tighten speaking
of quitting time when
the colored women filed out slowly
to have their purses checked,
the insides laid open and exposed
by the boss's hand.

                            But then she laughs
when she recalls the soiled Kotex
she saved, stuffed into a bag
in her purse, and Adam's look
on one white man's face, his hand
deep in knowledge.

ELLEN BANNISTER

Timid Family

We're a timid family.
Our dogs are ashamed
in front of other dogs.
We crack eggs open carefully,
fearful of the shell. We
run our fingers through
the yolk, searching
for a trace of bird.

We're a timid family.
We save our tears in little
blue bottles and bury them
in the yard. We dry our
socks in the attic.

We never barter. We
pay the check quickly
and leave without speaking
to anyone.

Four churches bound us.
Four churches, five prisons.
We can't get away
from the singing.

If you visit us,
don't be surprised.
My father will leave
the room, and my mother
will hide her book
under the coffee table.

MARCUS CAFAGNA

Something Faithful

When my Aunt Eleanor's throat was scarred
by the blade of a knife, I wasn't there.
But it's the pain and itch

of healing I can't imagine, the years
of ruffles and turtlenecks until she
allowed it to be seen

at family gatherings. In something
low cut the scar was a deep red
valley into which I couldn't

look. Still she's never accused
my cousin of madness or blamed
the heroin he tried to kick

with Quaaludes. She only ducks
her chin at times, says
it shows a mother and son

can live separate
lives since a scar is something
faithful, a way her skin

will never give him up.

The Way He Breaks

When I separate the blinds today
I watch the dark-haired kid
across the street, shooting baskets
hard with both hands. He's had it
with the Crisis Center. The aluminum
backboard shudders each attempt,
the ball most often rolling the rim
but not dropping through. He's pounded
rubber over cement too many days,
over battered painted foul lines,
dribbled and faked his way between
imaginary defenders. No one there
when he finally makes the shot.
What holds him to this place?
What act of bad luck?
Who might he miss when suddenly he
pauses, frozen in Olympic posture,
focused on the hoop, the missing net,
as if something has just occurred
inside him that makes all of this
some kind of rotten joke? The way
he breaks from that—sprints
into the highest jump
like someone drowning,
pushing his weight
up off the bottom.

Five Verses

I.

Ajax only addressed Zeus as Sir,
Now Ajax is a toilet cleanser.

II.

I thought I saw a Greek goddess.
Turns out it was a man in a dress.

III.

Jehovah: We bring good things to life.
Jason: Take my wife, please. Take my wife.

IV.

Nike, no one can run as fast as you.
I got it. Your name. Written on a shoe!

V.

Though the Trojans were gullible,
                    and the Athenians won,
Don't enter another's body
                    without wearing one.

JACQUELINE BERGER

Grandfather

Did you leave Bialystok
because you were draft age,
because pogroms rampaged your village,
because living with a brilliant older brother
was unbearable?

Whatever exists in imagination
exists in reality,
when your brother wrote this
years earlier
no one could imagine his death
at Auschwitz
or yours in Los Angeles.

Those first years here
did you think of your parents,
angry at them for letting you go
knowing they would never see you again,
did you walk the streets of Chicago
with some private agreement
to go on?

My young lover feels this way
in the room he shares with his brother,
eight months in this country,
not happy or sad, he prefers
to work hard and forget
the country he left and the war
that makes it impossible to return.
I put his dick in my mouth
and he shuts his eyes and smiles
as any boy smiles at good news,
at a letter from home.

If You Love Something, Let It Go

Homebound in a fuselage, tucked in, curled against you,
I watched God's words swim through black paragraphs
of the front page, ripples moving under a cloud's shadow.
A fortune fired up through my mind without my aid:

"Keep coming closer, kid, all should be well."
Once I'd come down, my babbling tongues
cut into by the secretary's flinch,
it hardly mattered if I lived or died.

I bore my tan cat to the gas chambers, I
who'd raised her to keep me up, flinging her
again, again, onto the wheat-gold floor.
She screamed all night to feel her four pads work again.

Hunched in her wire cage, screaming
down that hall, she screams in my dreams,
a secret friend I sing love lyrics to
who won't judge me from beyond me,

can't interrupt, want sex, or leave
language, a curled child buried
under the warm floor of a clay hut,
sheltered in the family's endless love.

Preen into this muddy fishpond I've inherited.
My mind. They say koi thrash around
down here, their gold wedding band mouths
gulping through the brown skin

when your forefinger taps knowingly.
In my neighbor's yard, he's ripped up
ivy tresses, revealing benign cactus tentacles
crisscrossing his dirt plot. Their one root,

we still can't find. Is breath a nest
between my hot heart and that raven paused
against me? Its skull keeps cruising
around this way, that way, famished

in the flyless air, its pecker
sharper than the beak between
my too-probing eyes, its black bod
lighter than these bloated bones,

its feathers sweating, gorged on evening heat,
glinting in the sunset as if faceted,
a coal ghost still inside a diamond,
its brand new neon body electric being broadcast

on the black screen of these closed lids.
Burst me open, love, to life's dark dove,
that shadow clumped around
a wing-wrapped shadow,

stumbling up to this thumb and forefinger pincher
outstretched, offering these inky fingerprints,
that deadly little loved one flitting off
in awkwardness, in blessedness.

Commencement Ode

Fellow loser, there's no future?
Even the Bee Gees suffered in a world of fools,
staying alive.

So wear green pants,
sing foolishly, and dance
upon the grave of Andy Gibb.

Sweet spoiled sixteen, I got
from our broke pop
a band of gold. Now that he's

pawned, the half-drowned glint
in its star sapphire's skyblue
blinds like a blade.

Touch me, neighbor, staring
down at shaking finger shielding
these shut lids: I'm half-hiding, my forelobe

bowed, attention curling up through dark meat tunnels,
scooting home across the black sea in this skull,
lost in Death's deflated star from even you.

Hear my stereo? On this front porch, I rise
from my knees, shoulders stooped, these plucked wings
spanning open to engulf the world's deep love.

I kick the door open behind me, sing softly
along, mixing up the words to vinyl prayers.
A squad car's blue light strobes away.

Turning inward, back into our living room,
I feel the TV's heaven—lapis screen flinch
as I ram this throbbing soft spot into life.

A Costume Straitjacket's Black Sleeve in Armoire Shadows

1.

Hiding from this life of murder
in a one-room nest of tan adobe
granted to him one wild summer,
the spoiled creator, bowing

like a found pilgrim, leans
into a Frigidaire. This erect
coffin's trapped starlight
chills looking glass eyes,

numbing nerves in fingertips
snatching an iced apple,
lifting one last Bud Light,
his prints flayed off.

2.

Before bedtime, his pen mislaid, he raised
his skin-thin mattress for the first time,
exposing a whirlpool of black spiders
to the lamplight, then his scream;

dreams failing to come, he felt them swirling,
vacuumed up again into his hindbrain,
his skull pounding the flabby pillow,
his deathmask imploding in sneezing dust.

Some other laughed. Blinds torn open,
he hanged his twitching frown out
through the frame containing this
targeted face, and there

3.

he was, inside the spilling lamplight's
center ring, the overhearer, squatting
on a squashed nest of scythed fennel,
his black leather jacket a prayer rug

spread out beneath his beak-sharp stare—
that girl-haired heavy metal drummer,
that starved trash practically fat
from stuffing his corpse plenty when it's free,

that Hollywood hustler who fucked drag queens
for the cameras, who hitchhiked from Tustin,
where his Mustang burst, to Taos,
a thirsty kitten howling in his pocket.

4.

Till it croaked. Face draped by a blond mane,
his snarl held back inside a twisted mouth,
his blue eyes silvery with sex, an Apollonian
Satan taking prey down,

he's doomed, of course, to thumb
into a knifeblade.
He hissed, "Don't you love leaving me
out here?"

That morning, on dust-gold streets, their eyes had hit;
the drummer's fist had opened, then
his palm had slid down, fingers fanning
across his own zippered bulge.

5.

"People out here," he hissed, "see
you're pretty crazy." The man wept,
go home, pirouetting his whole
body into its dark hole.

He paws his guest bed.
Cassette tapes clack.

He slaps his choice into its silver weapon.
Its voice box. Forever

hungry, keeping his trap locked,
dancing in the night against himself,
he'd howl as if wanted,
dead or alive.

CLAUDIA RANKINE

Plain Talk

The sky kneels close to the earth
like a voice becoming intimate
and turns him restless in their bed. This is why
he finds her awake, framed by the doorway,
ironing at midnight. Following
the iron forward, back, forward, he watches,
hopeful—tomorrow what was familiar will be familiar
again—though tears open into the blue fabric.
At their wedding she wore white;
the dress cascaded, its lace hem like leaves
against the floorboards. He remembers
holding her profile up to the future—her face,
the same rich brown of mackerel beside his
like a promise settling as earth upon earth
in the unlit hills of marriage.
Now he feels like a man evolved
from the unnatural landscape of a dream.
He knows it is not that she doesn't, she does
seek within herself the path out, tries hard
to trim back their vows to this,
the only possible life.
Shaking the shirt out, she frees the heat
against her body as if heat
could comfort on the worst of nights.
And hers is only one kind of existence:
tightening the belt around his robe,
sucking gently his lower lip,
he gathers himself close before turning
back to bed, trusting the ruby-throated morning
to provide her passageway.
For it's only her dreams that taunt her,
widening her eyes in darkness, blending

the untroubled night with her restless sorrow.
And how could he, forgiving her lack of ease,
collect her from her indigenous darkness
and lead her again to the resting world?
With what words could he summon her?
There is so little urgency in plain talk,
how could he simply say, *Sweetheart,
don't. Not to yourself. Not to me.*

GALE NELSON

Ode

for Alison

The discontinuity rescinds the longer-
lined format of dexterity in such a manner
that thieves themselves warn
the ombudsman to shrink-wrap
the artichoke hearts in gulleys.

Have you seen the larger–than–life portrait of kittens?

Shame is golden hue. The bitten conformity
should never vent the clipping, yet
the lacking cut-out form is negligible.
Have you been to the mountain spring
to sip on rocks, or did you burnish the ends
as they stood taller than grief?

The first box is the lavender. The orderly
fellow has a bin near the door that disturbs
my aesthetic pleasure of collective growth.
And the sounds of a rotund baritone
when egalitarian novels supper on parasites.

Shat upon in the lesser queen-driven cat.

This then answers the question of what
happened to the beetle.

Glory, glory, the deadly sins
are forgiven once you have eaten
at the other man's restaurant.

And the anxiety of arranging
the tour is alleviated by the tonsil-cure

being performed this very minute
on the orphan by his father.

Could we gather enough evidence,
we would be summoned
by gravity itself to perform
the latter parts of the hymn,
learned in childhood, memorized again
as adults, and sung with vigor by
a mother and her progeny in the front
room, with an instructor of foreign languages.

To marginalize even the liquid substance
that could not have hampered our approach
to the governmental bins,
this masquerade was developed
by a glutton, by a simple order of flopping
tug boats, and a wheel axle, greased.

Touching base with squiggles. A tapestry
not for blinding my eyes, if you please.

Shoring up. Lateral movement a pair
of brightly colored long-necked bears given
away as the leaf motif flows concurrent to paling.

Keys and a heritage of treatment. Reason
with me this natural conviviality, vex the larger
candle that has been diminished by contextual use.

Hold the book properly, hold it between
your left index finger and your ear, so as to
better view the paper clip under the shackles.

The return of the monkey is not
a very mechanical act. The star is
not a ledger or a favorite animal in postures
resembling those taken by boxcar-riding bankers.

A long piece of rankled steam
pouring forth on the last trailer.

This is where I come to plunk a couple
of plans into the hearth. Hear this idea—
the fabulous jab is neither for nor against
the passage to the central core. It is merely instrument.

Read longer the ampersand than the simple
spelling out of *and*, and that is where we differ.

I am more of a stumble-bum when it comes
to an uncomfortable theorem on moles
being the first animals to quit playing
tennis for the lake shore crowd.

Cowardly, shame-facedly, the lynx develops
its sea-going attitude when faced with
genetically trained seals playing games
with small squirrels in a parlor room in
the better part of town.

Shucks, the trio was gored by a raft of
historically correct amphibians.

See you soon, listlessly sitting below the
foraging birds, nesting in a wicker cup
of pavement. Silence as a porridge gush.

I have, I have that, I can make a copy. Oh
tears in an olden rubber chair, grated
with nethering pictures, fallowing.

Sub brine.

With every color option, we harbor
a fortitude known by the locution experts
as speech. So then, we absolve the visual,
we discontinue every use the peeling
could have had, and risk normalcy.

Also, thank you for the gig. I had not anticipated
such germinated wires running through the
fifteen or fewer conclusions that may have

whispered more often were they not so
bored.

Aviary, avuncular, these just stand-ins for what
was meant. Does that mean that emotion is for
the moment dead? If so, where can the figs sign
up to dance at midnight?

I change my response, you hold fast. We've given
more thought to this unkeyed inclination, and
pansies will often bloom this way.

Why the locking up what I have never
seen? Should distances be traveled in the
larger scene, then let us contempt-wise eat
our supper with the orator leering poolside.

When the bottom sewn.

A gallery of partridges fattened up on crumbs.

Eat, we say, wish yourself to consume
these lovely bits of mush. Mash a corn
and scrape an inner ear, then eat, eat.

Palliative advertising campaign runs risk
of shooting ducks in foot. Audience survey
reveals ignorance backfires as shadow—
sylva parade has gone awry.

Why bend at the wrist the hand, come
hold sham ketchup in a paper sieve
that has just begun to leak.

Are we really giving them a recent
kiosk to blow up to demonstrate
danger in the new world order? Then
give them mine, and eight of yours
before reading to them the larger points
made by scholars of the Eighteenth Amendment.

These lavender chocolates, had you tried
many of them before deciding to invest?

Again, the queen-driven cat. . .

Water, a two-dollar clock, a situational
guitar, a week's worth of books, a self-
starting vocabulary, and a gross of pencils,
all sharpened.

The eggs are not to be peeled off the tapestry
until after the curator returns. And that goes
for the ones that stink, too.

Bequeath me with artichoke hearts, or at least
the ever–so–ordinary beetle. And, if you wouldn't
mind, pails and sand for carrying on about weather,
the latest being not to my particular wet-veined
liking.

SHARAN STRANGE

How To Teach Them

I. GROOMING

Maybe she saw God the Father lurking
behind each seven year-old's face—
thirty pairs of eyes watching her, judging.

For twenty-odd years the same crop of bad
& good—their mamas, uncles, cousins.
So many ruined. Insolent. Unkempt.

Thirty offspring every year,
she never wanted to push one
out of herself. What world

could they have outside her own?
How to teach them that happiness
would come only from acceptance,

that beauty begins with cleanliness.
Her classroom was as orderly
as her childless home.

II. BEAUTY

TV pageants had taught us
how to line up, be sorted.

I pitied the boys who had to pick us.
They must've seen those contests too.

What we saw had everything to do
with love, the promise of it.

The screen was a greedy mirror
withholding the goods,

reflecting our hunger. Desire
& denial, at once, our ration.

At school we rehearsed adult dramas,
learned that our bodies could betray us.

Our teacher urging each one,
the boys chose eagerly,

shunning the dark, the moving
lips, the pleading eyes.

Snow

It came once, the year I turned
ten. That year I learned how
I would become a woman & began
my monthly vigil. But this was
the miracle, singular, unexpected.

The whites had finally stopped
resisting. Unwanted at their school,
we went anyway—*historic*, our parents
intoned, eyes flashing caution
to our measured breaths.

That first martial autumn mellowed
into a winter of grudging acceptance
& privately nursed discontent, a season
of hope shaped by fists & threats.
Then angels molted, pelting all

of creation with their cast-off garb.
We went home early, drifting through
a landscape of sudden ghosts,
the yard churning in frothy waves,
as if by an invisible tide of protestors.

What I remember most is its rude
coldness, stinging & wet. How we
mixed it with milk, sugar, vanilla,
into a poor child's ice cream which
melted before we could savor it.

JILL GONET

And Other Fantasy Lovers

A space determines and fills with narratives.

A person offers another person a role
and the other person hands one back.

One constructs a network that fills in with definitions.

One is a map with various color pins in various locations.

One believes words are acupuncture points and enough
poems will heal us.

One becomes dislodged from her role, from her network.

The outcast floats in anguish, trying for all the world
to find a pin to settle on
but there is nowhere to land—and the present
is continuous, and a becoming is always a question of how to be.

◆

When this one was very young
Shetland pony provided a motive for desires and demands,
for narratives of what a day could be and what
a summer could be. But another child
won the raffle.

One was left fantasy, a continual supply
of necessary beasts in answer to some enormous questions
that huddled on the periphery like boulders rolled
to the edge of a pasture.

Sometimes out of sight, sometimes to be climbed and from which
to view the horizon of a childhood.

◆

To be, to build something.
Pressures and intensities squeeze one into vertiginous areas of documentation.

A space fills with its time, with collections of artifacts
from moments spent in concrete attempts, colors and shapes
arranged in a pleasing succession, according to plans
of where things are shelved and how things are stored.

The human spirits zoom through, at the mercy of so many possessions,
on the way to dispose, or acquire more.

They provide a something to settle upon: crates and crates,
for instance, of books, stacked like prayers against terror.

◆

One has removed pins from the map and replaced them
or found others to put in new locations. One particular pin,
when pulled, moves the others too.

One draws it out slowly; it affects the entire rest of the landscape.
It becomes irresistible to play with pulling it
so the others begin to fall.

One wheels in a frenzy over the map, deciding one moment the map
was the world, it was everything,

deciding next day it was small and confining.

One turns the pin another quarter turn and sees the others falling more.

Questions of value filter through and permeate every hesitation.

One doubts.

One must let them fall where they may
and begin to search for a new contour to the pasture
where that pony, so long desired,
could frolic and be adored.

One Rose

Down from the street I descend
to a cluttered wicker jungle.

Baskets of tangled branches,
decorative arrangements, for sale

for those desiring indoor flora.
I see buds of blood perched

on slender stems. Gravity bends them
slightly, clustered in a frosted case.

The man with an accent asks me,
trying to patch things up with a lady?

Not quite, pal. And if anyone asks,
you never saw me before. Got it?

That's all. One rose. A blind pulse
of blood sent out by a heartbeat.

If only it knew where it came from
and why it was going to where it was sent.

REUBEN JACKSON

Steps

You may not think about it now,

but someday you'll
be at a party,

(If you can find one that
fits Daddy's curfew)

and our family
name will be questioned.

You know how he
and Martin Luther King feel
about fighting,

but your rose petal in an April breeze
step

will probably incite laughter,
and what if I am not around?

So we tried.

My feet resembled his
at the outset,

but found themselves
pirouetting toward distant cities.

Even then,
I lived in fear of laughter.

It has taken
more than an evening
to love spring.

ELIZABETH ALEXANDER

Four Rounds from "Narrative: Ali"

6.

There's not
too many days
that pass that I
don't think
of how it started,
but I know
no Great White Hope
can beat
a true black champ.
Jerry Quarry
could have been
a movie star,
a millionaire,
a Senator,
a President—
he only had
to do one thing,
is whip me,
but he can't.

8. TRAINING

Unsweetened grapefruit juice
will melt my stomach down.
Don't drive if you can walk,
don't walk if you can run.
I add a mile each day
and run in eight-pound boots.

My knuckles sometimes burst
the glove. I let dead skin
build up, and then I peel it,
let it scar, so I don't bleed
as much. My bones
absorb the shock.

I train in three-minute
spurts, like rounds: three
rounds big bag, three speed
bag, three jump rope, one
minute breaks,
no more, no less.

Am I too old? Eat only
kosher meat. Eat cabbage,
carrots, beets, and watch
the weight come down:
two–thirty, two–twenty,
two–ten, two–oh–nine.

10. RUMBLE IN THE JUNGLE

Ali boma ye,
Ali boma ye,
means kill him, Ali,
which is different
from a whupping
which is what I give,
but I lead them chanting
anyway, *Ali*
boma ye, because
here in Africa
black people fly
planes and run countries.

I'm still making up
for the foolishness
I said when I was
Clay from Louisville,
where I learned Africans
lived naked in straw
huts eating tiger meat,
grunting and grinning,
swinging from vines,
pounding their chests—

I pound my chest but of my own accord.

11.

I said to Joe Frazier,
first thing, get a good house
in case you get crippled
so you and your family
can sleep somewhere. Always
keep one good Cadillac.
And watch how you dress
with that cowboy hat,
pink suits, white shoes—
that's how pimps dress,
or kids, and you a champ,
or wish you were, 'cause
I can whip you in the ring
or whip you in the street.
Now back to clothes,
wear dark clothes, suits,
black suits, like you the best
at what you do, like you
President of the World.
Dress like that.
Put them yellow pants away.
We dinosaurs gotta
look good, gotta sound
good, gotta be good,
the greatest, that's what
I told Joe Frazier,
and he said to me,
we both bad niggers.
We don't do no crawlin'.

TORY DENT

Listen

In your prison, your ochre cell, big as a couch, you toss on the cot and read the same poem on the ceiling, on the walls of your brain and heart and watch drop by drop the mist bead up cold and damp on the porcelain toilet next to your head where you're forced to sleep with the symbol that epitomizes your prison life and therefore your life in toto it seems, the conclusion the all encompassing pain that spreads throughout your body like a generic formation, down to your toes, which if pointed and bare would graze the bars when the guards pass, their heels on the cement execute a torture all their own, the brass rings of their keys, that bob against their waists like an Indonesian earring, tease with a kind of hideous and addictive music, as if listening to the keys, to the chime of them together with such intensity, you can almost hear each one individually and find the one that is yours, as if listening to them could let you out, give you the power to open your cell effortlessly like a drawer; listening, listening, you walk through the village of corridors and notice, oddly, how your heels sound differently than the guards', notice how odd it is that you have time to notice the change underfoot from institution to courtyard, the sun suddenly thrown on your head like a burning blanket, listening to the burning; your shirt catches fire, you fall in love with fire, walking from city to forest, listening to the leaves burning, to the trees burning too, to the rain sad and cool and feminine that relieves you in the smallest way at first, pinpricks your face and then, as if letting go at last herself, soaks your shirt, your pants, your hair, your hands, as you approach with no specific direction but with this strong sense of destination into the thick of the forest, the way you would enter a church and heading toward the altar as if pulled by something magnetic and good, toward the sweet gate and iron cross hung at an angle, Christ's body bowed like a sail, you turn to measure how far you've come, when abruptly you behold a couple making love on the velveteen pew and listen surreptitiously to their breathing like keys, to the chime of them together with such intensity you can almost hear each one individually, hers short and warbling, his long and raining, and thinking of rain remember that your clothes are dry now inside the soft stones of the church, and comforted, you inspect without method, though meticulously the architecture, the rafters, the stained glass, the tall brass tubular columns of the organ, the eyelets on the altar cloth, listening to the various creaks and cracks amidst the polished wood so quiet, and then as if increased in volume to only the breathing, hers short and warbling, his long and raining, and yours yours as you hold her writhing in your arms, entering her like a church, her hair falling in your face, like fire her hands sad and cool like rain splayed against your face, like keys loosened from their ring, like an Indonesian earring, listening to the music hideous and addictive and magnetic and good.

Poem for a Poem

for Jade

And the snow fell lightly in Cambridge
where I swallowed the lightning of you whole,
a bolt with such a hyperbolic zig zag to its edges
that it seemed cut out of cardboard for a school play.
It stayed that way, stuck inside me like a pipe,
a spine of bite-sized bones.
And the snow fell lightly in Cambridge
where I stood on the platform in public for you,
you placed precariously before me like sheet music,
just paper, I know,
but not outside of me as I had hoped,
as I wrote that winter in those black mornings.
And the snow fell lightly in Cambridge.
My lamp snowed whitely on my desk, a street of snow
where white mice multiply by the hundreds.
And everything was so cold, all my animate objects,
except for the lead of my pencil, a welding utensil
or flashlight to guide my exodus in the snow.
I wrote you, a wagon I pulled on the road
in the effort to leave you, to let you go.
Or maybe it was more the other way around,
the words, breadcrumbs strewn to lead me back home.
Does it matter, really, which direction I desired?
I built, plank by plank, the rope bridge with so much purpose
that the purpose became the purpose in itself:
the relief of the labor of mindless work,
the stinging panic that brought lovely focus
to the next cliff. The next cliff
was all I thought about,
as if sailing in a ship at dawn.
And the snow fell lightly in Cambridge.
So whitely it put me back in my days,
the hotel décor as monochromatic as my thoughts
of you, you the poem, and the you in the poem,

the two merging together like a photograph
when a matte finish snapshot is what I have left.
The landscape behind the amateur portrait
landscapes the landscape of my pain, rank with weeds
outlasting of you, or me, as landscapes do;
though as a landscape of snow you'll always loom
where the lamp light on my desk whitely snows.
I thought because you were so complete,
because you came out whole like a baby
or twelve foot snake yanked from my gullet,
great sword of Excalibur ripped from its stone,
that at last you were separate from me as a landscape.
But deeper you sank instead, absorbed into my liver
like a bottle of vodka I'd consumed.
Now there's no getting rid of you.
I could tear you up, burn you, stubbornly disown you,
sign a pen name in the place of my own,
and still you'd roll through my head, a motion picture
sway below me still the sturdy net I weaved of you that winter.
I even feel guilty and somewhat fearful
as if you had the power to paralyze my hands,
break every bone in my fingers like a king
draw and quarter me for my traitorousness;
then turn all my poems to mush, as if they be, by the grace
of god, not already that.
And with the spiteful vengeance of a jilted lover
ensure supernaturally that they never be read,
for they're not made of the pure substance of you,
like the real thing I shot up my veins,
and let the much talked about bliss run rampant
not caring, not caring about anything.
Ironically I wrote you to make myself clean,
a thousand baths taken in the writing of you,
the symbolic cleansing of a baptismal crucifix.
Now you riddle me, permanently, bodily, a body tattoo,
internally ruinous, a virus and not just deadly
but deadening to all other poems and men.
Everything breaks down to the denomination of you,
everything I write simply the dissemination of you,
replicating in my body. O my molecule.

The Inner Life

Today I dare to claim the unnamed,
the deep febrile inner life

I slough off each month, loss that's
one less life gravitated to earth,

no matching sets of x and y,
chromosomes not to build their life

in me, not yet. I'm not yet sad
for that loss, feel no remorse

to wash your seed from me, rinsing
away its scent, the heat I've come

to love, your signature inside me
trailing off to disuse. So much

of what we have we don't use,
content to let our bodies go

only so far before we pull back, out,
stopping to watch each other, take

each other in. Yes, I'm muscle and sinew,
cartilage, artery—yes, my body is gaining

and losing, just as yours is gaining
and losing, our potential seemingly

infinite, as we could not wear away,
never leave behind bones becalmed

and drained. This is chemistry:
this mixing and turning, diminution

of cells and waste, a lessening
I know each month as damp, secret.

Not out of shame now, but out of awe,
I carry this secret, feel allegiance

to the jazzy mechanics of birth, its names—
Fallopian tubes, ovum, uterus.

I can hum these names to myself,
steady against the pain, cramps

pulling deep strings across
the belly. I can chant

this inner life, feel its tension
and release, constriction and ease.

And I can give that life to you,
knowing it safe from ridicule,

knowing it can grow one day
into inestimable riches, wealth of birth.

Good Humor

In our neighborhood of run-down houses,
of abandoned lots and corner groceries,
nothing tasted better than ice cream's

sweet delight: the delicate peaks
and swirls of vanilla soft-serve,
the cold chill of Italian ices

scraped from their containers
with tiny wooden spoons—cherry
and rainbow staining teeth, gums.

How we loved orange push-ups
that melted down our fingers,
so sticky we couldn't help

licking our thumbs and fingertips,
palms grasping at the slippery
treats. Remember the red, white

and blue bomb pops, sugar
and color frozen on a stick,
popsicles almost too heavy

to handle, almost too large
for the child-mouths that
welcomed them, sucking until

the colors faded, until
pallid ice was left behind.
All the flavors we could want

lived in the white truck
that cruised our streets
on summer afternoons: coconut

and chocolate, strawberry shortcake
and lemon–lime, peach and succulent
pineapple pulling us through

those heavily humid summer days.
We'd listen for the faint music
of that truck, wrangle dollars

and quarters from parents,
grandparents, and line up,
one behind the other, ready

to cool our tongues, freeze our teeth,
longing to lick and swallow everything
that melted beneath the summer sun.

Nijinsky's Winter Afternoon, With Faun

I started to write a song about love, then I decided
to write about you. I'm always giving people things
they don't want. You were talking
about Heidegger, your lips shaped cold air into a breathlessness
between us, your startlingly detailed
equivocations. I've been trying to write about violence
for so long. A week of traffic jams and fog
filtered through glass, the country crumbling
in my restless sleep; old men in plaid jackets on the corner
drinking quart bottles of Old Milwaukee; the color black
again and again. My first summer in Boston
a bum glanced up from tapping at the pavement
with a hammer to whisper "Nigger," laughing,
when I passed. I'd reached the age of reason,
I suppose; my body was never so clean again. Some afternoons
I can see through you to the rain, writing your name
in fine black silt. There is no third person;
the same lines substitute for snow with which the lake effect
shrouds a half-abandoned rust belt
city, white and still unmarked and falling
all night: some drift taking your place. I was just
scribbling again. *Take it from me,* my stereo claims, *some day
we'll all be free.* If anyone should ever write that song,
the finely-sifted falling light.

ALICE ANDERSON

Girl Cadaver

Sitting on the carpet of your LA room, crying, you tell me
of the girl whom you don't love whom you slept with

because you do love me and you were so lonely. New York,
you say, is very far away. Your room is filled with all

the parts of your new life, piles of notes and stacks
of anatomy books with photos of the dead, skinned

or sliced open, the bodies split up the middle, a few stray
pubic hairs still attached at the thigh. I can only

flip through the glossy pages a few minutes, skipping
the section on reproduction, before feeling full inside.

I haven't seen you in almost a year, a year since the night
you drove off like a flame in your blue truck, screaming

You're nothing to me, just another girl, just another fuck.
At night, with you, in bed again, I pull the pillows

over my head, clinging to the edge, falling into dreams
of my body, cut up and bloody, hanging from ropes

in trees above the front yards of all my ex-boyfriends.
Today you tell me about Gross Anatomy, about

accidentally severed breasts, and your girl cadaver,
the one you were so lucky and happy to get before you found

her brain so soft and rotted it slipped between your fingers.
Shit, you said then, about her. You joke that if I were

to leave my body to science some med students, after
the initial joy at a cadaver so young and thin and

(why did you assume it would be young?) with just a few
nicely healed scars, would open me up, find things missing,

the liver destroyed, that thick womb, and say, *Shit.*
We listen to Patsy Cline and you say *I like women's voices.*

And so when again I tell you I love you I think of my brain,
imagine it soft as rotted peaches, the color of my perfume.

We make love again and behind my closed eyes I picture you
slicing me open, quiet and swift, expecting to see just organs,

just tissue, just blood. And I see your face, dark and still
and damp, grow panicked and wild as all of your children

slip out of me, scurrying between the pages of your books.

MAUREEN ADAMS

Gatherings

(Episodes of Work)

◆

You. Pittsburgh. Rolling old-fashioned cigars. I find this picture folded
in your shirt. Leaning into breasts on worktable. Electrical cord tied
in knots hangs low bulb onto your work. It is 1921.
Italian stories. These tables are full of you.

◆

Old Spinner in a Georgia Mill.
I was so small doctor said,
        "Give Pug a chew of tobacco"
That was gonna make me grow. I just laid down
on that porch and vomited like a dog.
Didn't stop—Give me a dip of snuff, maybe it
won't make me sick—but it did. Still I kept
dipping it a little longer 'til I got to where
I dipped it regular. Then I started to grow.

        I got a mind to ramble but I don't know where to go

◆

Song of the Shirt. New York City clothing worker.
Now, I've never envied Mill people, but I heard my
daughter Mavis say she wished she could slim
into one of my numbers, and go swimming at the shore.
I do piece work in a shop.
Sections of the floor do handwork by climates.
Northwing does the wool lapels; Eastwing does
the shirt collars; Southwing doing waistbands;
and the West, we're bathing clothes.

I slipped my daughter home a beach trunk—
wore it through the halls of our building.
No fit beach, or time to go to it. Just bare legs
up and down the stairs.
But, working the Mill, I hear there's plenty of Ocean Time.

◆

Tire and Rubber Co. A small woman was seen out there
(a dress-maker and trained nurse) who might have
passed anywhere (Akron, Ohio) in a crowd without
notice, but was behind the recording of secret
meetings through second-class mail.

Wild Women don't worry, Wild women don't get the blues

◆

Big Mary and her Army. Overalls and Snuff.
Raised rolling pins, fire pokers, bed posts
to drive off the scabs.
        The Bosses were pulling something called
        the "Southern Strategy"
        clap slap trap keeping Wobbly workers out
        That's when we moved
        in up and all over those non-Union.

This Union Maid was wise to the tricks of the Company Spies

Wives breathing—Sisters across—Mothers outside

All closing in on many points surrounding the Charleston district
Hungering for that chance in.

◆

You said you were going to dress them all like Eva Peron.

My grandpop lived with us, he made coffins.

Laundresses found jobs elsewhere.

We lived in Cabarrus County, you know.

Long before day, just before day, just comin' day, just about daylight, good light, before sunup, about sunup, sunup.

Innumerable feminine skills were needed to set the farm table.

My husband told me about the Bolshevik Idea. I'm standing in front of the stove, he's sitting in cigar clouds and deep chair.

I'd quit working around July to have my babies, then would go back in September. My Summer Feeding.

Teaching adult literacy in Boston. I wasn't considered a preacher.

Folding paper boxes in those long skirts. Strict part, thick knuckles.

Locked shops. No Union in, no worker out. 143 died in that fire. I was watching from the street, all those women jumping out of the burning windows.

Our boss told us there would be no OPEN CLASS WAR.

◆

Stumbling across traces of coercion
Why all the bodies washed up under bridges?
    (Missouri, Delaware, St. Charles)

    My brother was shot. He couldn't get work
    for a year because of organizing.
    Government ripped our place apart.
    Friends found him dead in a train yard after
    some meeting outside Chicago.
    "Out of county" they said, "anyhow, he was
    acting lawless" My husband is a doctor,
    he looked at the wound, could tell the bullet
    entered from behind. Probably running for the
    train out.

    He was an old time hop-picker, I'd seen his face before
    And I knew he was a Wobbly by the button that he wore

◆

If a man decides to deliver a message lying flat atop a freight car
he must strip his loyalties of place.

    You see, the informants were called one-eyes.
    Always had a sneer and bad work because half
    the body was always watching us. Even gave
    their time for eating a half-ass go at.

Conduct plus suspicion lends panic to the one-eyed plowboy.

Thanks to *The Little Red Song Book* and Ma Rainey and Bessie Smith for lyrics in
italics—M.A.

Hunt in Couples

the eye has a tendency to close when watching branches burn along
the edges of pear orchards

this county is not accidental   one told other of its rumored plenty
overheard on a walk through a barren span of land

squeeze lemon onto the opened avocado to stop the browning
chew the slices while moving past miles of fruit trees   it's only bad on the
first taste   such symmetry these farmers have   grouped tight   put to seed

today the prison labor moved off   trailing behind the portable toilet
hooked to the bumper   work a day off a sentence with every 10 hours
along the freeway   put them in school buses that sit idle on weekends

one watches other work in the trees and vines all summer
stained fingers rubbed clean in the thick outdoor water cooling in the
same metal tank the milking cows drink from   one covers other's
burnt head with a damp towel as they move back to the room   they
are given stiff straw hats for the days that follow

one explains to other what is known of the long wave along the ocean
basin other calculates in days when the next El Niño will hit   they
plan to be in Baja up to their knees in salt water to feel it pass

one installs screens against the valley insects   other sleeps it off
unroll the wire mesh into long sheets as other moves under the dreams
of water containers strapped to backs and the stacking of berries—
continually pushing the round imperfect fruit into piles   one nails the
pieces of screen to the open spaces between ceiling and baseboard   a
fall from the bed becomes an afterthought   other wakes into the space
of sound between the strike of the hammer and the noise of contact

other is out among the fruit as one picks through the lot behind the Carpenter's Union Hall   scrap wood, glass jars, pieces of rolled copper, railroad ties, plastic food containers, clumps of animal hair snagged on thistles, hay bailing wire   several trips are made back to the room   stacked on the front porch one waits for other and today's peak crop

September heat brings broken branches, cracked soil, movement West vines curl down as the desert air migrates under the guise of seasons   air caught in the deep valley, trapped stagnant in this bowl   first one carries other, then they switch   arms coiled under the damp curve behind the knee   hanging upside down across the length of back one reaches into other's pocket for the last of the fruit

LENARD D. MOORE

Collards

I am watching my sun-filled garden
scented with onions I will dice
and cook in the pot of collards
I will eat later this evening,
or I could leave them to search
with their burrowing roots
for my great-grandmother.

I was just a child
when in her glowing last years
of living alone,
she taught me how to use a hoe
against dry earth,
how to pull collards from their beds,
and how to prime the pump for the water,
that nurtured the collards' green widening.

What I need is this land to continue
providing me what grows, what shapes
into the nearly grown-up plants: collards,
crisp, sweet, and beautiful,
under a summer-blue sky.
I have unraveled like that leafy vegetable
rooted into ash-black earth,
here where everything becomes kin
like shadows that merge with one another,
dark shapes lengthening with the greens.

MIRIAM LEVINSON

Geology, Summer 1983

We're hiding from the sun,
the whole young lot of us, but we can't hide
from the heated bars of iron between us
pulling together, pushing apart
here in the Colorado with our socks off.
We've followed it down, this river reigning
over stone, digging its way down
to befriend the underbelly rock lying in wait
for so long. Now we stand
facing four billion years,
our mindless feet cavorting on bones of things
that swam here, on their dried-up shit
and fallen teeth, hanging out.

Michael and Tom spotlit prance and splish–splash
shirtless like fags, flip their wrists,
knowing their chests ripple, skin brown
and soft even still,
that they are young and beautiful
and make us laugh. And Gary, my sweet friend,
you watch too but you love men and it must burn
          into you.
You will confess it
to Michael, later to me,
you want–love–him–want–love–
me, a bizarre triangle will form
struggling, digging through these layers
of sandstone and shale,
metamorphic folds.

That's it in spades.
Laid down by vanished ocean currents

sand, silt, mud, animal bodies conspire
and harden. Blistering heat lifts water away
easy as raising sweat from my palms.
Then the pressure. Enormous pressure
creates a new, dangerous heat. Grains
and bodies melt together, buckle,
crystallize into
not predictable igneous molecule planes,
not neat sedimentary layers,
but a mutant, a mixed-up, beautiful
metamorphic monster.

And we
are melting,
dissolving,
layering, forming
something.

I'm still excavating it all.

About the Poets

MAUREEN ADAMS, 25, grew up in Central California and lived in San Francisco for six years before moving to Providence to attend graduate school at Brown. Her work has appeared in *Five Fingers Review, Central Park* and *The Bridge* (San Francisco State). **ELIZABETH ALEXANDER**, 30, grew up in Washington, D.C. She teaches at the University of Chicago and reviews books for *The Village Voice* and other publications. Her book *The Venus Hottentot* (1990) appeared in the Callaloo Poetry Series. Her poems in this issue are excerpted from her forthcoming Fisted Pick Press chapbook, *Narrative: Ali.* **ALICE ANDERSON**, 27, was born in Tulsa, but grew up in California and Mississippi. She continued moving on her own—to New York, Paris, Geneva, Milan and Osaka—and has stopped for the time being in New York. She's also moved around the arts—opera, jazz, piano, violin, ballet—but has found poetry the most expressive medium. Her poem in the issue, along with a forthcoming appearance in *New York Quarterly*, marks her first publication. **ELLEN BANNISTER** grew up in Leavenworth, Kansas. Her poetry has appeared in local publications. Currently a graduate student in Lawrence, Kansas, she is 23. **PAUL BEATTY** was born in Los Angeles and now lives in New York. **JACQUELINE BERGER**, 31, was born in Los Angeles and now lives just outside of San Francisco. A graduate of Goddard College, she also studied at Freehand Writers' Workshop in Provincetown. She teaches English as a second language to immigrants. Her work has appeared in *Northwest Review* and *Womantide.* **SOPHIE CABOT BLACK** was born in 1958 and grew up on a small Connecticut farm. Her influences include Emily Dickinson, Leonard Cohen and J. M. Coetzee. Her work has appeared in *The Atlantic, Antaeuss* and elsewhere, including *Best American Poetry 1993.* A collection of her poems is forthcoming from Graywolf Press in 1994. She lives in New York City and teaches with Poets in Public Service. **JAMES BLAND** received a B.A. from Vassar and an M.F.A. from Cornell, and is completing a doctorate in English at Harvard. He has received an Academy of American Poets Prize, a Bread Loaf Writers Workshop scholarship and MacDowell Colony residency. His work has appeared or is forthcoming in *Praxis, Callaloo, Key West Review, The Windless Orchard, Kenyon Review* and *Columbia.* **MARCUS CAFAGNA**, 36, grew up in Detroit and Brooklyn. His work has appeared in *Poetry, Minnesota Review, West Branch* and elsewhere. His poem "A Mother From Brooklyn" won the Devil's Millhopper Press Kudzu Award and his book manuscript was a finalist for the 1992 Starrett Prize. He counts Sharon Olds—with whom he has worked at the Squaw Valley Community of Writers—as a major influence. He teaches at Michigan State University. Adrenaline-slut **THOMAS COOKE** enjoys hurling himself from Point A to Point B as fast as possible. His writing has appeared in *Two-Ton Santa* and is forthcoming elsewhere. **CHRISTOPHER DAVIS**, 33, grew up in Southern California. Texas Tech University

Press published his AWP Award-winning first collection *The Tyrant of the Past and the Slave of the Future* in 1989. TTUP will also publish a workbook of writing exercises he has developed while conducting an extracurricular poetry workshop for HIV-positive people, which he does in addition to teaching at the University of North Carolina at Charlotte. **TORY DENT**, 35, grew up in Connecticut and now lives in New York City, where she is pursuing a Ph.D. in English at NYU. Her poems have appeared in *Antioch Review, Partisan Review, Paris Review* and elsewhere, and her art criticism in *Arts Magazine* and *Flash Art*. Among her honors are fellowships from Virginia Center for the Creative Arts, Yaddo and MacDowell. Her book manuscript has been a finalist for numerous awards, including the Whitman, Bobst, National Poetry Series and Barnard Women Poets Prize. **THOMAS SAYERS ELLIS** grew up in Washington, D.C., where he attended Paul Lawrence Dunbar High School. His writing has appeared in *Agni, Callaloo, Graham House Review, Hambone, In the Tradition: An Anthology of Young Black Writers* and *Ploughshares*. A founding member of the Dark Room Collective, its reading series and literary journal *Muleteeth*, he lives in Boston and works at Harvard's Carpenter Center for Visual Studies. **PAJA FAUDREE**, 25, grew up in Memphis, Tennessee, though also lived in Scotland and Hungary. Currently unemployed, she has been a nomad after completing her M.F.A. in poetry and playwrighting at Brown. Her philosophy background and her experiences in biological and medical labs are among her strongest influences. This is her first appearance in a literary journal. **EDWIN FRANK** lives in New York City. His poems have appeared in *Grand Street* and the *New York Review of Books*. **JODY GLADDING** was born in 1955 in Pennsylvania. For the last six years, she's lived in Vermont and worked at Bear Pond Books in Montpelier. She received an M.F.A. in writing from Cornell, where she studied with A. R. Ammons, and was a Stegner Fellow at Stanford. Her first book, *Stone Crop*, has just appeared in the Yale Younger Poets Series. **GABRIELLE GLANCY**'s work has appeared in *Paris Review, New American Writing, American Poetry Review, Kenyon Review* and *The High Plains Literary Review*. In 1990, she as awarded a New York Foundation for the Arts fellowship. In addition to writing both poetry and fiction, she is translating a book by Marguerite Duras—half of which appeared in *Fiction*—and one by Jean Genet. Born and raised in New York City, she now lives in San Francisco. Born in 1960, **JILL GONET** grew up near New Bedford, Massachusetts. Of her poem in this issue she writes, "Periodically we reinvent ourselves or perhaps only our mythologies about ourselves. This poem is a record of a life breaking open in order to reinvent itself." Despite upheavals, she has made Seattle her home for the past eight years. Her poems have appeared in *Best American Poetry 1992, Ploughshares, Antioch Review, Black Warrior Review, ZYZZYVA* and elsewhere. **SUSAN HALLAWELL**, 26, grew up in Marblehead, Massachusetts, and now lives on the East End of St. John, U.S. Virgin Islands, where she works as a bartender and volunteers as a sailing instructor. She has an M.F.A. in poetry from the University of Virginia, where she was a Hoyns Fellow. Her work has appeared in *North American Review, Southern Poetry Review* and *Tar River Poetry*. **REUBEN JACKSON**, 36, was born in Augusta, Georgia, and has spent most of his life in Washington, D.C., where he now works as an archivist with the Smithsonian's Duke Ellington Collection. His work has appeared in *Chelsea, Indiana*

Review, Catalyst and The Plum Review and in his first collection, fingering the keys (Gut Punch Press, 1991). He loves poetry a great deal, but would give it up in a second if he could sing like Marvin Gaye. **ALLISON JOSEPH** was born in London in 1967 to parents of West Indian ancestry. She grew up in Toronto, Canada, and the Bronx. Her book What Keeps Us Here (1992) was the first winner of Ampersand Press's Women Poets Series Competition. The collection also received the John C. Zacharis First Book Award from Ploughshares and Emerson College. She lives and teaches in Little Rock, Arkansas. **SUZANNE KEEN**'s poems have appeared in Agni, Chelsea and The Ohio Review. She teaches poetry and the English novel at Yale University. **ARNOLD J. KEMP**, 24, was raised in Boston. He is a graduate of Boston Latin School, Tufts University and the School of the Museum of Fine Arts. He now lives in San Francisco, where he works as an arts administrator. He has received several awards for his poetry, including one from the Academy of American Poets. His writing has appeared in Three Rivers Poetry Journal and Callaloo. A show of his visual art recently was held at the San Francisco African American Historical Society. **JOSEPH LEASE**'s poems have been published in Paris Review, Grand Street, Agni, Pequod, Boston Review (featured and with an introduction by Robert Creeley) and elsewhere. He has new poems forthcoming in Grand Street and Colorado Review. **MIRIAM LEVINSON** is a 25-year-old Bostonian who grew up in Livingston Manor, New York (population 1,500), graduated from Yale, and now works in the marketing department at Beacon Press. She hopes the influence of W. C. Williams, Sharon Olds, Li-Young Lee, Rita Dove, William Carpenter, good haiku, and photographers Garry Winogrand, Robert Frank and Helen Levitt occasionally peeks out between the lines of her work. This is her first contributor's note. **PETER MARCUS**, 34, was raised in Great Neck, New York. His poems have appeared or are forthcoming in Poetry, North American Review, Poetry East, Yankee, Yellow Silk and elsewhere. He considers Sharon Olds, Galway Kinnell, Robert Hass and Brenda Hillman his main influences, though he only sees them one week a year at the Squaw Valley Community of Writers. He is completing a Ph.D. in clinical psychology, specializing in counseling Native Americans and individuals with eating disorders. He lives in Arizona. **CHRISTOPHER MILLIS** has had his work published in Seneca Review, New Letters and The Missouri Review. He authored the libretto for "The Magnetic Properties of Moonlight," which appeared at Dance Theater Workshop in New York. **LENARD D. MOORE**, 34, grew up in Jacksonville, North Carolina. He has been influenced by stories told to him by his parents and grandparents as well as haiku, jazz, blues and gospel music. His work appears in Callaloo, North Dakota Quarterly, Obsidian II, African–American Review, Colorado Review and The Haiku Anthology. He lives in Raleigh, North Carolina, where he is Writer–in–Residence for the United Arts Council of Raleigh and Wake County. **HARRYETTE MULLEN** is the author of Trimmings (Tender Buttons) and S*PeRM**K*T (Singing Horse), both available through Segue Distributing (New York) and Small Press Distribution (Berkeley). She teaches African–American literature and creative writing at Cornell University. **LAURA MULLEN** was born in Los Angeles in 1958 and raised in various parts of California by various sets of parents. "House," one of her poems in this issue, was inspired by a visit she paid with Carol Snow and her husband to his parents' house on the Olympic Peninsula, during which she wrecked Carol's car, among other things. She is the author of *The Surface* and part of the M.F.A. faculty at the University of Miami. Author of *stare decisis* (Burning Deck), **GALE NELSON**, 32, is coordinator of the Graduate Program at Brown University. He was born in Tarzana, California, and lives in Providence with his wife, fiction writer Lori Baker. **CARL PHILLIPS** was born in 1959 and grew up on a series of air force bases. Among his influences are Li Po, Gertrude Stein, Cicero, Tacitus and all the ancient Greeks—reminders, perhaps, from his days as a Harvard classics major. After teaching high school Latin for nearly a decade, he decided to take writing a bit more seriously. His collection *In the Blood* (Northeastern University Press) won the 1992 Morse Prize. He was the 1992–93 Starbuck Fellow in poetry at Boston University. **CLAUDIA RANKINE** was born in Kingston, Jamaica, in 1963 and raised in New York City, where she now lives. She graduated from Williams College and the Columbia M.F.A. program. Her work has appeared or is forthcoming in *Kenyon Review, River Styx* and *Southern Review*. **REGINALD SHEPHERD**, 29, was born and raised in New York City. He graduates from the Iowa Writers' Workshop this spring. Among his major influences are Wallace Stevens, W. H. Auden and Jorie Graham. His work has appeared or is forthcoming in *Antioch Review, Callaloo, Kenyon Review, Green Mountains Review, Massachusetts Review, Poetry, Verse, Southwest Review, Poetry Northwest, Western Humanities Review* and elsewhere. **SHARAN STRANGE** grew up in the South and among her many influences are writers who have some affinity, geographically and existentially, with that place. She notes, "My poems investigate memory, the shadow that fall between act/experience and expression." Her recent works appear in Callaloo and In the Tradition. A member of the Dark Room Collective, she has been a MacDowell Colony fellow. **NATASHA TRETHEWEY** was born in Gulfport, Mississippi, in 1966. She received a B.A. from the University of Georgia, an M.A. from the Hollins College Writing Program, and is now at work on an M.F.A. at the University of Massachusetts at Amherst. Her work has appeared in *Callaloo, Seattle Review, First Things* and various anthologies. **KEVIN YOUNG** holds a Stegner Fellowship in Poetry at Stanford for 1992–94. His work has appeared or is forthcoming in *Callaloo, Kenyon Review* and *Graham House Review*. A member of the Dark Room writers' collective in Boston, he is also co-founder and publisher of Fisted Pick Press, a fine-press poetry chapbook series.

♦   ♦   ♦

HANNA MELNYCZUK

On the Verge: Emerging Massachusetts Artists

John Berger's meditations on Vermeer's painting "Painter in his Studio" (*Pequod* 28/29/30, pages 11–16) led me to think more deeply than I ever had before about the difficulties of the jurying process. Our first response to a piece is far from our final, and not always our finest, one. Sometimes we need to let a work come to us taking small steps. This ought to happen naturally. Berger's description of Vermeer's painting and his analysis of it caused me to remember the *time* required in grasping, understanding and feeling a piece of artwork. The jurying process, as it is practiced today (indeed, as it was practiced by this feature's curators: Gerry Bergstein, Mark Booth and I) is not natural. It's based on instinct and reactions to reproductions of the real work. One is asked to respond quickly, sensitively, ruthlessly. And yet within the confines of time and despite the difficulty of this task one goes deep within oneself and searches for that voice which conveys to us our feelings about what is before us in that instant.

The only criteria we had when we decided to organize "On the Verge" was that the artists selected were from Massachusetts and that they had no gallery representation. We looked at all five slides by each of the 144 applicants anonymously and we voted, also anonymously, until we reduced the pool of candidates to 30.

At this point we began discussing the work. We selected an eclectic combination of 11 artists who were indeed on "the verge" of something new, and whose work was strong, promising, and met our intuitive criteria.

After the selection process was completed, I left to teach and travel in Ukraine. When I returned to Boston last September I learned that one of our curators, Mark Booth, had left the Artists Foundation where the show was originally scheduled to go up that November. The Foundation, along with the rest of the world, had fallen on hard times. May they pass, and quickly.

Since we'd postponed the show a number of times already, I decided to seek alternative quarters. After many phone calls and much slogging around Boston, and with the energetic help of Jan Collins, the work found Peter Barnes with his wonderful openness and his fine ambitious new Gallery Equus at 125 Kingston Street, in Boston. That's where the show will be held during the month of April, 1993.

The Artists

The eleven artists were asked to describe their work. I have taken salient aspects from their statements which I thought might help in appreciating and understanding the work in the portfolio.

Elaine Corda does installations which use domestic settings and materials that portray ". . . how time and life pass us by, marked by our simple daily repetitiveness."

Death and disease have impacted Dennis Crayon's life for the last five years. He has lost friends to AIDS, cancer and addiction. Through his work he "expresses the powerlessness one feels when disease is controlling his life and leading him towards death."

Michael Dwyer has dedicated his time to creating art which is public, participatory, site-specific, recycled, and environmental or any combination thereof." In his statement Dwyer writes: "Statement? Are we not all creative beings? Can art change the way things are? Can humans change the way they themselves are? How do we make art a part of our everyday lives? Where does the artist end and the viewer begin? Who is reading this?"

Jane Ehrlich describes her work: "I am striving to create images which harken back to a prehistoric realm, a timeless place that comes from the unconscious evoking the passionate, fecund and angry aspects of my inner being. Drawing from my inner wellspring, and women's own emotional history, my work refers to the beginning where an ordering, nurturing spirit forms the underpinnings of everything we know."

Lyn Feakes describes her recent series of wall sculptures and installations: "I have been exploring the interactions and relationships among our bodies, our homes and nature. The wall sculptures are cabinet-like and utilitarian in format, reminiscent of furniture. The cabinets also contain references to our physical selves and the passage of time. I see wallpaper and fabric patterns as an attempt to reconstruct nature into a format suitably benign for the home. One of my interests is to shift the context of these floral motifs to reveal a more complex, perhaps darker, account of our relationship to nature."

The paintings created by Beverly Floyd deal with " . . . an obsession for connections, for the relationships between people and the natural world, between people as nature and people as nature's enemy. It is a way of discovering natural incongruities and pointing to the existential bridges that bind them together. My work is driven by conflict and contradiction, not as a way to resolve it, but as a way to illuminate the dualities of existence."

Lydia Nettler's collaborative installation with Harriet Diamond was described as "exploring the movement of drawing from a more depictive form to a more abstract form. Her drawings begin as panoramic views of river and woods and end as drawings of swirling water and rock forms. In a certain way Nettler moves into the river taking her audience with her. The last area of the installation, drawings of dark water and rocks with gravel and a simple rock form on the museum floor, is derived in part from the Japanese rock garden. The transcendence of nature and nature's ability to remove the consciousness of self as apart from the whole is one of the themes recurring in Nettler's work."

The sculptor Venae M. Rodriguez works with polarities: aggression/vulnerability, rigid/fluid, male/female. She writes: "I choose materials that relate tension and fluidity and create forms that have both masculine and feminine qualities. Forged steel is the structural element, in opposition to more vulnerable or precious materials such as plastic wrap or gold leaf. Each piece is at odds with itself: seductive, biting, fragile and ferocious."

Photographer Amanda P. Swain describes her process: "It is important when I am photographing in a new place to divorce myself from all that is familiar. I imagine myself to be a tea bag with no properties of its own, that has been given time to steep, to become saturated with the truth of the space." She describes the places she chooses to photograph as ". . . sacred because for thousands of years the land has been used as a place for prayer and ceremony. Before I pick up my camera I must let my arrogance dissolve; and work through my own fear that the place summons up." Her "Verge" photos were taken in Queensland, Australia, where she was working on a documentary project on aboriginal communities.

For Keith Walsh, "art-making is anecdotal: it is a semantic reconstruction and communication of personal life experiences. These works are based on psychological states I have encountered while driving cars, watching television, carrying a briefcase full of information, and laboring and meditative activities such as sawing wood, building crates, writing, typing, drawing, speaking and sleeping."

Susan White describes her piece "Lolita's Daymare" as being "inspired by the Nabakov masterpiece *Lolita*; it attempts to convey the brutal yet queerly fantastical consequences of a childhood gone awry. The coffin shape of the piece suggests the possible irretrievability of self resulting from abuse and neglect. One might peer into and beyond its interior to find a glass pendulum suggestive of time passed and passing, difficult though magical. The coffin surface is built up from layers of colored dies and waxes, partially cut away by surgically precise instruments. If one were to characterize the healing process of the soul it might look like this: not a simple delaminating of accreted time, but a cutting into time, and a gradual though imperfect consolidation."

ELAINE CORDA

"Vanity with Seat," 1991
mixed media, 61" × 46" × 66"

DENNIS CRAYON

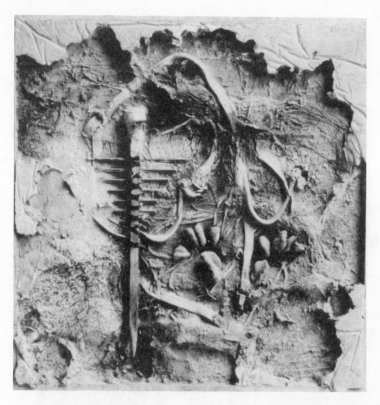

"9/12/91," 1991
plaster, wood, pigment, spray paint, rubber, metal, 36″ × 36″

MICHAEL DWYER

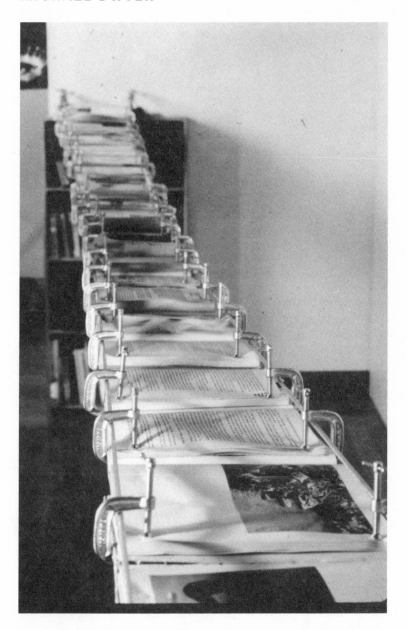

"BookBridge," detail from "Eggroom," 1992
interactive installation

JANE EHRLICH

"Approaching Storm," 1991
oil on paper, 13" × 19"

LYN FEAKES

"Untitled," 1991
oil on wood, 24″ × 30″

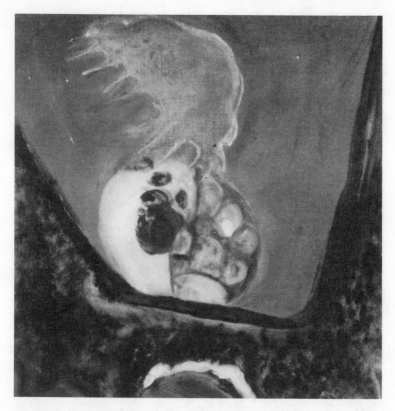

"Untitled," 1991
distemper, oil on linen, 24" × 24"

LYDIA NETTLER

"River, River Passage," 1991
charcoal on screen, 100″ × 180″

VENAE M. RODRIGUEZ

"Place of Things Beginning," 1992
forged steel, gold leaf, 29″ × 37″ × 57″

AMANDA P. SWAIN

"Pansy–Possum's Feet"
Tribal Elder from Kowanyama Aboriginal Reservation;
Cape York Peninsula, Qld. Australia, 1992
photograph, 11" × 14"

KEITH WALSH

"Could," 1992
charcoal and acrylic on canvas, pylon, rubber, text, tape recorder loop

SUSAN WHITE

"Lolita's Daymare," 1991
steel, plexi, wax, aniline dye, 42″ × 17″ × 28″

About the Artists

Born and raised in Massachusetts, **ELAINE CORDA** graduated from the School of the Museum of Fine Arts in 1990. In 1991 she received the Clarissa Bartlett Traveling Scholarship. She has spent most of the past year in Tucson. **DENNIS CRAYON** was born in upstate New York in 1956. He studied graphic design at the University of Buffalo and graduated from Boston's School of the Museum of Fine Arts with a fifth-year diploma in 1992. **MICHAEL DWYER** is currently living in the Pocono Mountains of Pennsylvania. He is working as an art facilitator for children, as a journalist for two local newspapers and as a member of the Way-Off Broadway Theatre Company. **JANE EHRLICH** was a Massachusetts Artist Fellow in Drawing in 1982 and 1989 and received the Museum School's Traveling Scholarship in 1989. She has shown extensively in the Boston area, including shows at the MFA, as well as the Fitchburg, Fuller, Danforth and DeCordova museums. **LYN FEAKES** was born in Boston and now lives and works in Somerville. She attended the School of the Museum of Fine Arts and received an M.A. in Geology from the University of Oregon. **BEVERLY FLOYD** was born in Houston, Texas, in 1949. Her work has been shown nationally in both private and university galleries. She received a B.F.A. from the University of Massachusetts and an M.F.A. from Yale. She teaches at the Guild Studio School in Northampton, Massachusetts. Painter **HANNA MELNYCZUK** is currently an Artist–in–Residence at the Griffis Art Center in Connecticut. **LYDIA NETTLER** studied art at the Museum School and has exhibited widely. Born in New York City, she now lives in Northampton, Massachusetts, where she works as a psychotherapist. **VENAE M. RODRIGUEZ** grew up in a large family in Washington State. She lived in Seattle for several years where she worked in ceramics. At the age of 26, she transplanted to Boston to study sculpture at Massachusetts College of Art. She plans to attend graduate school this fall. **AMANDA P. SWAIN** received her B.F.A. in photojournalism from Tufts University and the Museum School in 1991. Among the projects she is working on is a photographic documentary of aboriginal and white Australian culture, for which Polaroid Corporation awarded her a substantial grant. Born in New York in 1963, **KEITH WALSH** now lives in Somerville, Massachusetts, and works as a shipper. He received a B.F.A. from the University of Hartford, Connecticut, and an M.A. from Tufts University. For the last few years, he has been pursuing a blend of visual arts and semiotics. **SUSAN WHITE** was born and raised in North Carolina. She received an M.S. in Fine Art Conservation and was the Frohlich Fellow in Objects Conservation at the Metropolitan Museum of Art. She is now sculpting, painting and performing.